# The World of
# Cinema

Christopher Kenworthy

## EVANS BROTHERS LIMITED

Evans Brothers Limited
2A Portman Mansions
Chiltern Street
London W1M 1LE

Editor: Nicola Barber
Designer: Simon Borrough
Picture research: Victoria Brooker
Production: Jenny Mulvanny
Consultant: Colin Harding, Curator of Photographic
Technology at the National Museum of Photography,
Film & Television, Bradford, UK

First published in 2001
Printed by Grafo, Spain

*For Millie, the next film fan
generation in my family*

British Library Cataloguing in Publication Data
Kenworthy, Christopher
World of Cinema
1. Motion pictures - History - Juvenile literature
I. Title
791.4'3'09

ISBN 0237520389

VISIT OUR WEBSITE
www.evansbooks.co.uk
Evans

**Warning**
Some of the films listed
and discussed in this
book are certificates PG,
15 or 18 and therefore
not suitable viewing for
younger readers.

## Acknowledgements

Cover (middle left) NMPFT/Science and Society Picture Library (centre) J. S. Library International (far right) Charlie Chaplin™ Copyright
© 1999 Roy Export Company Establishment (bottom left and page 90) TM/© 1999 Estate of Marilyn Monroe by CMG Worldwide Inc.,
Indpls, IN marilynmonroe.com (bottom centre) Ronald Grant Archive Back cover (top) www.corbis.com/Mitchell Gerber (top right,
middle and bottom) With thanks to Image FX Animation. Pictures by Rod Ebdon page 7 Ronald Grant Archive page 8 (left)
NMPFT/Science and Society Picture Library (right) © Méliès page 9 (right and page 87) J. S. Library International (bottom) © Walt
Disney Enterprises, Inc page 10 Werner Forman Archive page 11 Science Museum/Science and Society Picture Library page 12
NMPFT/Science and Society Picture Library page 13 (top) NMPFT/Science and Society Picture Library (bottom) NMPFT/Science and
Society Picture Library page 14 www.corbis.com page 15 The Ronald Grant Archive page 16 (top left) NMPFT/Science and Society
Picture Library (bottom) NMPFT/Science and Society Picture Library page 17 (top) ©Lumières (bottom) The Ronald Grant Archive page
18 (top) © Méliès (bottom) The Ronald Grant Archive page 19 The Kobal Collection page 20 (top right) www.corbis.com/Massimo Listri
(bottom) The Ronald Grant Archive page 21 The Ronald Grant Archive page 22 © D W Griffiths page 23 (top) Charlie Chaplin™
Copyright © 1999 Roy Export Company Establishment (bottom) © Hal Roach page 24 (top) © MGM (bottom and page 91) The Ronald
Grant Archive page 25 (left) © BIP (right) The Ronald Grant Archive page 26 © Association Chaplin page 27 (top) The Kobal Collection
(middle) © MGM (bottom right and page 91) J. S. Library International page 28 The Ronald Grant Archive page 29 NMPFT/Science and
Society Picture Library page 30 J. S. Library International page 31 www.corbis.com/Austrian Archives page 32 (all pics and page 86) ©
Eon Productions page 33 © 20th Century Fox page 34 (top and bottom) © Paramount page 35 (main pic) ©20th Century Fox (inset) ©
Paramount page 36 J. S. Library International page 37 J. S. Library International page 38 (top) The Kobal Collection (bottom) © 20th
Century Fox page 39 © Hammer Films page 40 J. S. Library International page 41 © Paramount page 42 (top) J. S. Library
International (bottom) © United Artists page 43 © Zoetrope page 44 (top) © Polygram (bottom) www.corbis.com/Craig Aurness page
45 The Kobal Collection page 46 (top) © UFA (bottom) © Riama page 47 © Spectra Films page 48 © Daiel page 49 (top right) J. S.
Library International (bottom left) The Ronald Grant Archive page 50 (middle) www.corbis.com/Jeffrey L. Rotman (bottom) © The
Government of west Bengal page 51 (top) The Kobal Collection (bottom) The Ronald Grant Archive page 52, 53 © Walt Disney
Enterprises, Inc page 54/55 Pictures by Peter Millard. With thanks to all at Telemagination page 56 © Walt Disney Enterprises, Inc. page
57 (top) © Walt Disney Enterprises, Inc  (bottom) © Dreamworks page 59 (top) © Aardman Animation (bottom) © RKO page 60 (top) ©
Prana Film (bottom) Corbis/Everett page 61 (left top and bottom) With thanks to Image FX Animation. Taken by Rod Ebdon (right) J. S.
Library International page 62 © 20th Century Fox page 63 © Universal page 64 Carlton UK Television page 65 © 20th Century Fox page
66 © Universal page 67 The Ronald Grant Archive page 68 J. S. Library International page 69 www.corbis.com/AFP page 70 (top and
page 88) © Goldcrest (bottom) J. S. Library International page 71 © Disney Enterprises, Inc. page 72 www.corbis.com/Hulton-Deutsch
Collection page 73 © Warner Bros page 74  www.corbis.com/Adam Woolfitt page 75 © Touchstone page 76 (top) © Coralco (bottom) ©
Walt  page 77 © 20th Century Fox page 78 www.corbis.com/Jim Sugar Photography page 79 © New Line page 80 © RKO page 81 (left)
© AMPAS ® (right) www.corbis.com/Mitchell Gerber page 82 (top) The Ronald Grant Archive (bottom) The Ronald Grant Archive page
83 (top) Sony Imax Theatre (bottom) BFI London

Every effort has been made to trace the copyright holders and we apologise in advance for any unintentional omissions.  We would be
pleased to insert the appropriate acknowledgement in any subsequent edition of this publication

# CONTENTS

# INTRODUCTION

*"Young man, you can be grateful my invention is not for sale, for it would undoubtedly ruin you. It can be exploited for a certain time as a scientific curiosity, but apart from that, it has no commercial value whatsoever."*

*Auguste Lumière, pioneer of cinematography, 1895*

From the beginning of time, people have tried to portray the things they saw around them in a realistic way. In places such as Lascaux, in France, Stone Age people took advantage of the natural bumps and shapes of the cave walls to make their paintings of animals look round and life-like. Later, painters used perspective to bring their paintings to life. However, the most perfect representation of life is a picture in realistic colour that moves and behaves just like the person or the animal it is meant to represent.

This book is a guide to the history and development of moving pictures from the very first photographic plate that held an image to the huge Imax cinemas and multiplexes of today.

Chapter one deals with the search for a way to make realistic images move. In chapter two, there is an outline of the history of Hollywood and an explanation of how the 'star system' developed. Chapter three looks at some of the many types or 'genres' into which films can be divided.

Chapter four is a brief tour of national cinemas throughout the world, a reminder that while Hollywood and its products dominate the English-speaking world, there are other, busy and important

*A three-strip Technicolor camera (see page 29)*

*Georges Méliès'* Voyage dans la Lune (Journey to the Moon) *(see page 18)*

studios that serve other lands and other cultures.

Chapters five and six are more technical. They look at animation, the way cartoons are made, and the technical wizardry used by the movie-makers to create special effects on screen.

Finally, in chapter seven, the work behind the camera comes to light. The army of unseen people and organisations needed to bring pictures to the screen is examined, as well as the way the industry sells its movies to the public.

*Clint Eastwood as the 'man with no name' (see page 42)*

*A scene from* A Bug's Life *(see page 57)*

# 1 FIRST IMAGES

The earliest known shows featuring moving action used cut-out puppets to make shadows. In medieval times, these shows were popular all over the Far East, but puppets from Java were especially admired. The puppets used in shadow shows were flat so that they cast a clear image when lit from behind. They were cut from thin leather, which could be painted and made to throw a coloured shadow. Each puppet was articulated beautifully so that the arms and legs could move independently. The operators, who moved the limbs with sticks, stood at one side of a white screen. Behind them was a bright light which threw the shadows of the puppets on to the screen. The audience sitting on the other side of the screen could see the shadows and the sticks – but not the operators. Skilled operators could handle two puppets at a time.

Shadow shows came to Europe in the 18th century when, in 1776, a shadow theatre opened in Versailles, near the palace of the king of France. The theatre was so successful that another one opened in Paris eight years later.

*A shadow puppet from Java. The shadow plays in which these puppets appeared often lasted all night, and were based on ancient Hindu epics such as the* Ramayana.

*This diagram, made in 1754, shows how a* camera obscura *works. Light travels through a pinhole (labelled V) into a dark room to create an upside-down image (labelled H) of the building on the right.*

# PROJECTING IMAGES

Early devices for projecting a realistic image were often ingenious. From the 16th century onwards, the *camera obscura* (meaning 'dark room') became popular in Europe. It was based on the principle that if light enters a dark box or room through a tiny hole, an upside-down image of the scene outside appears on the opposite surface from the hole. The first *camera obscuras* were light-proof, portable boxes. They were used by artists to throw an image which was then traced on to paper to produce working sketches. Some of the later *camera obscuras* were complete rooms in which one or more mirrors were often used between the hole and the opposite surface to make the image appear the right way up.

# OPTICAL TOYS

Early scientists used mirrors and lenses of various kinds to form images. The first projected image using a lens was from a device known as a magic lantern, invented by a Jesuit monk called Athanasius Kircher. We know that magic lanterns were in use in the 17th century because the diarist Samuel Pepys described one in 1666 with great wonder:

'Mr Reeves did also bring a lanthorn, with pictures in glasse, to make strange things to appear on a wall, very pretty.'

A magic lantern consisted of a lantern whose light was directed through a long tube like a gun barrel. The very first magic lanterns had no lenses, but a Dutch scientist called Christian Huygens developed the idea by putting a lens inside the tube to focus the light. Images painted on to glass were slid into the tube through a slot, and when the light fell through them, an upside-down image was projected on to a white wall in a darkened room. To make them appear the right way up, the slides were inserted upside-down. Magic lanterns are still used today, although they are now called slide projectors.

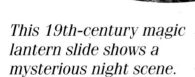

*This 19th-century magic lantern slide shows a mysterious night scene.*

# FIXING THE IMAGE

The first person to use light-sensitive chemicals (called silver salts) to preserve an image – and therefore the first photographer – was a Frenchman called Joseph Nicéphore Niépce. In the 1820s, Niépce found a way of fixing an image on a metal or glass plate coated with light-sensitive chemicals. The method relied on the reaction of the chemicals to light – but they reacted so slowly that it took the whole of an afternoon to take one picture. Niépce's partner, an artist called Louis Jacques Mandé Daguerre, took the process further and produced the first commercially viable way of preserving an image on a metal plate, called the Daguerreotype.

## OUT TAKE

Working in the 1830s, a British gentleman scientist called William Henry Fox Talbot developed a camera that took photographs on sensitised paper. He announced his process in 1839, the same year that Daguerre brought out his own much improved process. However, the photographs produced by the Talbot method appeared with the light and dark areas reversed. This is called a 'negative'. Talbot invented a way to print a true image (a 'positive') on light-sensitive paper.

# MAKE THEM MOVE

During the 19th century, many machines and toys were produced that appeared to make an image move. They all used the principle that the eye retains a picture of an object it has seen for a split second after the object has disappeared. That is why a flash of light in a darkened room remains in your vision even after the light has been turned off. This is called 'persistence of vision'. Scientists discovered that if they showed a succession of pictures of the same subject, each slightly different, the 'persistence of vision' convinced the viewer that he or she was watching a moving picture. This principle is the basis for all 'moving pictures', which actually consist of a series of still pictures, shown very quickly, one after another.

*A Zoetrope with a selection of picture strips. The strips were slotted inside the cylinder, and viewers watched through the vertical slits while the cylinder was gently rotated. Thanks to persistence of vision the little figures appeared to move.*

*The Praxinoscope was a variation of the Zoetrope which was invented by French artist Emile Reynaud (1844-1918). Viewers looked at the pictures in the cylinder through a mirror mounted in the centre of the device.*

Many of the early optical devices had exotic names such as the Zoetrope, the Phenakistoscope, the Thaumatrope and the Praxinoscope. These machines made pictures 'move', but they were limited in their interest. It was a British photographer, Eadweard Muybridge, who first thought of the idea of taking a series of photographs, one after another, in the manner of a modern-day strip of film. However, he stumbled across the idea completely by accident. At that time, there was a long-standing disagreement in racing

# THE WORLD OF CINEMA

*This strip of pictures taken by Eadweard Muybridge shows clearly the motion of the horse's feet and legs. After the first experiments, Muybridge increased the number of cameras to get even more detailed strips.*

**Curriculum vitae:** Eadweard Muybridge (1830-1904)
**Real name:** Edward Muggeridge
**Place of birth:** Kingston upon Thames, England
Muybridge was a strange and colourful character. He changed his first name to the original Saxon spelling, and then his surname in stages to Muybridge. In 1851 he emigrated to the United States, where he first took an interest in photography while recovering from injuries sustained in a stage coach crash. He became famous for his pictures of human beings and animals in motion, which are still used by artists today.

circles about the motion of a horse's legs while trotting. Some people said that the horse's feet all came off the ground together at one point, others that no matter how fast it ran, the horse always had one foot in contact with the ground. The legs move too fast for the human eye to see. Leland Stanford, former governor of California, asked Muybridge if he could settle the argument by photographing a horse trotting at speed. In doing so, Muybridge produced the first series of photographs in close sequence, like a very short strip of film.

Muybridge set up a series of 12 cameras next to a race track, each camera to be triggered by a trip wire. As the horse passed the cameras, it tripped the wires and fired the cameras, one after another. The pictures proved that a horse does leave the ground when running.

The controversy over Muybridge's pictures was so great that he had to repeat his experiment several times. It introduced him to a new technique of seeing how animals move, and he went on to photograph other animals, and human beings. At first Muybridge made his photographs into Zoetrope strips, but then he realised that he could show them to more people if they were projected. He copied his photographs on to a glass disc, which he then ran through a magic lantern, projecting them on to a wall. He called his instrument the Zoopraxiscope and showed it to great admiration at the Chicago World Fair of 1893.

## THE PHOTOGRAPHIC GUN

Making moving pictures by Muybridge's method needed a lot of bulky equipment. And while it is not too difficult to get human beings and animals such as horses to behave as you want, wild

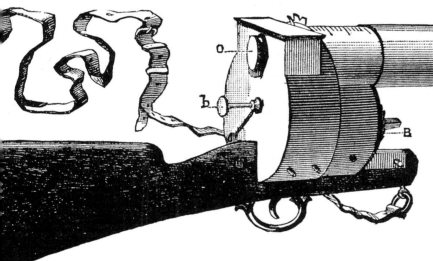

*Etienne-Jules Marey's 'photographic gun'. Marey used his device to take series of pictures of birds in flight, so that he could study how they flew.*

animals such as birds are a different matter. What wildlife photographers needed was a small, easily carried camera which would take a series of pictures, one after another. In 1882, French scientist Etienne-Jules Marey invented a camera he called a 'photographic gun'. It did indeed look like a gun, with a shoulder stock so that the photographer could hold it steady, a short, thick barrel which contained the camera lens, and the camera itself mounted in between. It could take photographs on a glass disc in 1/500th of a second. Marey was delighted, since he could now take 12 photographs in one second. This meant that he could photograph a bird in flight in the same way that Muybridge could photograph a horse at full gallop.

However, there is a limit to the size of a glass plate and the speed with which it can be changed. What was needed was some other method of recording the image. Rolls of light-sensitive paper film, brought out in 1885 by the American inventor George Eastman, solved this problem. In 1888, Marey showed a series of pictures taken at a rate of 20 per second on the new paper film through a camera he had himself designed.

*The internal mechanism of an Edison Kinetoscope, showing the 20-second film that passed above the projection lamp in one continuous loop*

# THE COMING OF CINEMA

In 1889, George Eastman first used celluloid for the backing of his films. Celluloid is a flexible, transparent material stronger than and as pliable as paper. The following years produced some weird machines, all aiming to capture a series of images on a strip of celluloid, but all using different techniques. One camera had 12 different lenses. Another used six different small cameras fixed to a rotating plate. The American inventor, Thomas Alva Edison wanted to record pictures in the same way that he had recorded sound. He put the work into the hands of his young Scottish assistant, William Dickson. During his experiments, Dickson was the first person to put little perforations in the side of the film to match a star-shaped cog wheel that fed the film through the projector.

Edison and Dickson made films for individual viewing machines called Kinetoscopes.

*A viewer bends over the eyepiece of an Edison Kinetoscope.*

## OUT TAKE

The first person to capture moving pictures of living people was a Frenchman called Louis-Aimé-Augustin Le Prince. Le Prince designed a camera which had 16 different lenses arranged in a large square, behind which were two rolls of light-sensitive paper. He used electricity to open the lenses one after another, and chopped up the resulting rolls of pictures afterwards, sticking the individual photographs together to make the film. His first film, taken with a single-lens camera, is the oldest known surviving moving picture. It shows people crossing a bridge in Leeds (1888). However, in 1890 Le Prince boarded a train to Paris and vanished, along with all his equipment. Nobody knows what happened to him.

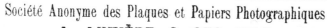

Société Anonyme des Plaques et Papiers Photographiques

**A. LUMIÈRE & SES FILS**

CAPITAL TROIS MILLIONS

Usines à vapeur : LYON-MONPLAISIR

COURS GAMBETTA, RUES ST-VICTOR, ST-MAURICE ET DES TOURNELLES

NOTICE
SUR

# LE CINÉMATOGRAPHE

AUGUSTE ET LOUIS LUMIÈRE

Imprimerie L. Decléris et fils, place Bellecour, 16, L
— 1897 —

*On 28 December 1895, Auguste and Louis Lumière (right) showed a film in Paris using their own camera-projector, the Cinématographe (above). The Lumières are usually credited with the birth of cinema.*

People paid a penny or a dime to peer through the eyepiece in the Kinetoscope and watch a short film unwind before their eyes. Then, in 1895 two French businessmen, Auguste and Louis Lumière found a way to show films to a larger audience. The Lumière brothers invented the first practical movie camera. They called their machine the 'Cinématographe', giving us the word 'cinema'. The Cinématographe also used holes in the film to ensure that it passed through the camera and the projector at the same speed. It was small and easily portable, and it took good pictures.

The Lumière brothers' first film, shown in 1895, was called *La Sortie des Usines Lumière* (*Workers Leaving the Lumière Factory*), and it is still amazingly clear and natural looking – except for the fact that the workers are all wearing their Sunday-best clothes and look very well rehearsed! Queen Victoria's Diamond Jubilee procession was filmed two years later in 1897, but the Lumière brothers' most popular film was *L'Arroseur Arrosé* (*The Waterer Watered*). It is about a gardener who is trying to water a garden while a naughty boy behind him keeps standing on the hose. Eventually, the gardener looks down the nozzle to see what has gone wrong – and gets soaked. The films were very short – about one minute each – so a session at the Cinématographe shows lasted only half an hour but included at least 12 films. Audiences were soon queuing down the street in Paris and later in London. The age of cinema had arrived!

*A scene from Georges Méliès':* Voyage dans la Lune *(*A Journey to the Moon*) which was based on the work of early science-fiction writer, Jules Verne*

**Curriculum vitae:** Georges Méliès (1851-1938)

**Place of birth:** Paris, France

Méliès is the father of special effects. Son of a rich shoemaker, young Méliès was fascinated by drawing and by moving figures. His father forced Méliès into his shoe factory where the young man was miserable until he realised he had been introduced to another of his life-long obsessions – machinery. After a visit to London where he became fascinated by magic acts, he sold his interest in the shoe business and bought the Théâtre Robert-Houdin in Paris, where he staged magic and variety shows. He tried to buy the Cinématographe machine from the Lumière brothers, but they would not sell. So Méliès went to Robert W. Paul in London who was making cinema projectors using Edison Kinetoscope films and, before long, film shows were a feature of the programmes at the Théâtre Robert-Houdin.

*Edison's tar-paper 'Black Maria'. The roof could be opened to allow the light in, and the whole building revolved to follow the sun.*

# THE BIRTH OF SPECIAL EFFECTS

The Cinématographe attracted the attention of a Paris magician called Georges Méliès. It was not long before Méliès discovered that the difficult tricks he had been performing on stage were more easily achieved with a movie camera. On stage, it took trap doors and some expensive machinery to make his assistant disappear. On screen, all he had to do was stop the camera, remove the assistant and start the camera again. The art of stop-action was born.

Méliès made a series of short films using special effects. For example, he filmed a conversation with a head that apparently swelled to enormous size by building a long rail track leading up to the camera. He mounted a box on a trolley which ran along the rails. Then he sat in the box with his head poking through a hole, and started filming while the trolley was far away, gradually cranking it towards the camera. The closer it got, the larger it became, with Méliès 'magically' chatting away. His film *Voyage dans la Lune* (*A Journey to the Moon* 1902), based on a story by Jules Verne, was a sensation.

# THE FIRST FILM STUDIOS

Méliès built his own film studio. Since at that time photography relied on natural light, the studio looked like a big greenhouse, lined with blinds and curtains to control the amount of light. In America, Edison and Dickson (see page 16) solved the problem of light in a totally different way. They constructed a huge box which was totally blacked out with tar paper, but with a roof that opened like the lid of a cardboard box. The New Yorkers, who were used to seeing big, black police vans, promptly called it the 'Black Maria'.

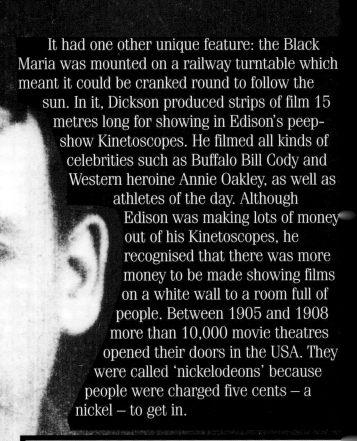

It had one other unique feature: the Black Maria was mounted on a railway turntable which meant it could be cranked round to follow the sun. In it, Dickson produced strips of film 15 metres long for showing in Edison's peep-show Kinetoscopes. He filmed all kinds of celebrities such as Buffalo Bill Cody and Western heroine Annie Oakley, as well as athletes of the day. Although Edison was making lots of money out of his Kinetoscopes, he recognised that there was more money to be made showing films on a white wall to a room full of people. Between 1905 and 1908 more than 10,000 movie theatres opened their doors in the USA. They were called 'nickelodeons' because people were charged five cents – a nickel – to get in.

## OUT TAKE

Many new techniques of filming were pioneered by Edwin S. Porter, one of the great innovators of the film industry. In 1903 he made a film called *The Great Train Robbery*. It combined exterior footage (shot out of doors) with the usual interior scenes; the camera 'panned' or moved to follow the action instead of remaining still; and there were close-ups and cross-cuts (see pages 21-2) between people and places. Most important of all, it involved a shot in which one of the cowboy bandits fired his gun straight out of the screen into the audience. This scene caused many arguments. Some people were deeply disturbed by it, some offended. But most audiences were thrilled – the idea of the thriller was born.

*At the end of* The Great Train Robbery *the gunman turns and fires his pistol straight at the audience. When this scene was first shown, people screamed with horrified delight, and some even ran out of the cinema.*

# 2 FROM SILENCE TO SOUND

At the start of cinema history, all movies were silent. At first, the novelty of the films was enough to keep audiences happy, and people often talked, cheered or jeered all the way through. In fact, movies were hardly ever shown in silence. Some were accompanied by a lecture, others by live sound effects. Some movie houses had a pianist to play suitable music 'live'. The film-makers issued lists of recommended music to go with films, but many pianists played their own versions. It was a cinema joke to have a sign saying: 'Please don't shoot the pianist, he's doing his best'!

The grandest movie houses had a full-scale organ which rose on a platform from a pit in front of the screen. The organist played popular music while the audience was waiting for the film to start, as well as accompanying the film.

*A staircase in the Tuschinski cinema in Amsterdam, which was built in the opulent 'art nouveau' style in the 1920s. Many cinemas were built in grand style, turning them into 'picture palaces'.*

## AN INTERNATIONAL LANGUAGE

There were advantages to making silent movies. Studios and distributors could show the same version of a film in any country without having to worry about audiences understanding what was going on. Producers could employ actors from any country, whether they could speak the local language or not. In films that required dialogue, the producers put in captions explaining the action when necessary. It was a simple matter to change the captions to suit the language of the country in which the movie was being shown.

Being silent did not prevent movies from being long and lavish. Italian film-makers became well known for making spectacular historical 'epics'. They used rich costumes, large casts with hundreds of extras, and big, expensive sets (the scenery in which films are made). As early as 1912, Enrico Guazzoni produced the first version of *Quo Vadis* which ran for more than two hours and was recorded on nine reels. It featured a full-scale chariot race.

*A caption for a silent film. Captions had to be short, clear and concise.*

*Quo Vadis* was followed the next year by *Cabiria*, in which for the first time the producer, Giovanni Pastrone, used a length of track to carry the camera smoothly on a shot. This kind of technique became known as the 'tracking shot', and it is still used today to keep up with anything from a slow-walking actor to a fast-moving car chase. It differed from Méliès' use of a track to create a special effect (see page 18) because the camera itself moved, as well as the subject.

*A tracking shot in progress on the set of the 1984 film,* A Soldier's Story. *In this scene, the camera and sound recordist follow the progress of the action between Howard E. Rollins (walking) and Dennis Lipscomb (in the Jeep).*

# A NEW STYLE OF ACTING

The most important film of this fast-moving time was made in the USA. It was *The Birth of a Nation* (1914) and was produced by David Wark Griffith (always known as D. W. Griffith). He was a pioneer in the movie industry, and is often known as the father of the modern movie.

Griffith used the cross-cut, a technique in which two events taking place in different locations are filmed and then interleaved with each other. It allows the audience to see that the two

*Confederate officers ride through town in a scene from* The Birth of a Nation. *This would have been a familiar scene to many of the older members of Griffith's audience when the film first came out.*

sequences are inter-related and happening at the same time. For example a sequence showing a police car chasing bank robbers often cross-cuts between the police and the robbers. Griffith also used close-ups, moving his camera as well as his actors. He built film sets so big they became landmarks. He was absolutely committed to his films – so much so that in one film he marooned his leading lady (Lillian Gish) on a real ice floe in a real river to get a particular shot.

Griffith seems to have been the first person to realise that the movie camera makes everything look larger than life. A fat person on the screen looks about four kilograms fatter. A casual wave of the hand looks on screen like a vast, sweeping gesture. Most of the actors who made films had been trained for the stage, so they were used to having to roll their eyes and pull faces to communicate with audiences at a distance. But the movie camera brought the audience to within a metre of the performer, and in some close-up shots, to within centimetres. To modern eyes, the performances of many early actors look ridiculous on screen. Even so, most directors encouraged melodramatic gestures because they helped to get the meaning over, even without the use of captions.

Griffith insisted on a more natural style of acting. *The Birth of a Nation* was set in the southern states of the United States, just after the American Civil War. The war had ended in 1865, only 50 years before the film was made. There were many people who remembered it and the misery it caused. This epic re-telling of those bitter years struck a chord with many American families. However, the film was openly racist and, while thousands of people flooded to see it, many others refused to have it in their cinemas, and some cities banned it altogether. Griffith went on to make many other films, but *The Birth of a Nation* was his footprint in cinematic history.

> **Curriculum Vitae:**
> D. W. Griffith (1875-1948)
> **Name:** David Wark Griffith
> **Born:** La Grange, Kentucky Griffith's father, 'Roaring Jake' Griffith, fought for the Confederates in the American Civil War. The Griffith family was made poor by the war and young David started his professional life as an actor with a wandering theatre company. He was not a success, so he wrote short films in which he also appeared as an actor. It was valuable training and he later turned it to great advantage, making hundreds of films.

# HOLLYWOOD:
# THE EARLY YEARS

Even while Edison, Dickson and Porter (see page 19) were busily breaking new ground in New York, something historic was happening on the west coast of the USA. In 1908, a film called *The Count of Monte Cristo* was made in California. This was the first film to be made on the west coast, and the area quickly became a centre for the movie industry. One reason was that

*Hollywood comedy kings Charlie Chaplin (top), Stan Laurel and Oliver Hardy (bottom). Laurel and Hardy's film* The Music Box *(1932) won an Oscar for its story which involves two men trying to deliver a piano to a house at the top of a very long flight of steps.*

movies were made by natural light, which meant they needed sunlight, and California was where the sun shone all day every day – or so it seemed.

The movie-makers were also driven west by the attempts of the big movie pioneers, headed by Edison, to control the industry through the Motion Picture Patents Company (MPPC). The MPPC was formed in 1908 by the pioneers of the industry to protect the legal ownership (or patent) of their films. Film producers were worried that there was nothing to stop the people who distributed and showed their films from making illegal copies and showing them without paying a fee to the producers. So the major companies formed the MPPC and announced that without their licence, nobody was entitled to produce, distribute or exhibit movies within the USA. The MPPC then established the General Film Company to distribute the films of its companies to licensed picture houses only.

The response of many independent movie-makers was to move west, far from the lawyers in New York. They looked for somewhere cheap and convenient in California and discovered a quiet, open farming area with orange groves. It was called Hollywood.

Film-making started in Hollywood in 1908. By 1910, the major movie houses were setting up business there. The following year, the first major studio was built and others quickly followed. By the time Griffith made *The Birth of a Nation*, 60 per cent of American films were being made in Hollywood. The location was perfect. Only a few kilometres away was the Pacific Ocean, ready to play any sea the producers wanted. A day's travel inland were the mountains and deserts now familiar in hundreds of Westerns.

Hollywood began to attract the people who were to become legends in their own lifetimes. One of the biggest areas for the cinema was comedy. Using special effects such as stop-action (see page 18), cross-cutting (see pages 21-2), and speeded-up motion, the great comedians were able to make their chases look funnier and their jokes more dangerous. The best of all of them was Charlie Chaplin. He invented the 'little man' in ill-fitting clothes who was always being bullied – but always won. Other comics included Harold Lloyd, who became famous for hanging from clocks and flagpoles high over busy streets – especially as he did all his own stunts. The deadpan Buster Keaton, the comedy team of the Keystone Kops (or Cops) and, later, Stan Laurel and Oliver Hardy all became hugely popular.

# THE HEROES

Just as popular as the comics were the action-man heroes of the silent screen. Men such as Douglas Fairbanks and Rudolph Valentino were almost impossibly good-looking on the screen. Fairbanks did all his own stunts and made his name as swashbuckling heroes including Robin Hood, the Thief of Bagdad, and Zorro the swordsman. Valentino starred in films such as *The Four Horsemen of the Apocalypse* (1921) and *The Sheik* (1921). When he died in 1926, at the age of 31, about 30,000 women queued up to see him lying in state, and the newspapers reported rioting.

By 1920, Los Angeles was well on its way to becoming the second largest city in the United States. Every young man who thought he had a good profile and young woman who thought she had a beautiful face packed a case and headed for Hollywood. The

*The smouldering good looks of Rudolph Valentino in* The Sheik *won many hearts.*

**Curriculum Vitae:** Douglas Fairbanks Sr. (1883-1939)
**Name:** Douglas Elton Ulman
**Place of birth:** Denver, Colorado
Fairbanks' parents separated when he was five, and his mother reverted to the name of her former husband which Douglas kept for the rest of his life. Trained in the Colorado School of Mines, he did a number of different jobs until he made his professional début on the New York stage in 1902. A star of the stage, he transferred smoothly to the screen and quickly became a firm favourite of the fans. When sound came along his stage-trained voice helped him to success. He was married for 16 years to film star Mary Pickford (see box). With her and Charlie Chaplin, he formed United Artists.

**Curriculum Vitae:** Mary Pickford (1893-1979)
**Name:** Gladys Smith,
**Place of birth:** Toronto, Canada
She started work at the age of five to help support her family. Billed as 'Baby Gladys', she toured with a theatre company and made her New York début at the age of 14, calling herself Mary Pickford for the first time. She broke into films two years later, working first for D. W. Griffith for $40 a week. Within seven years, she was earning $10,000 per week, and a year later could demand $350,000 for a film. Like many of the early stars, she was known by a nickname as 'Little Mary' but later went on to be 'America's Sweetheart'. She was so beloved as the shy, innocent young heroine that she played a 12-year-old even when she was in her mid-20s (in *Pollyanna* 1920). With her husband, Douglas Fairbanks (see box) and comedian Charlie Chaplin she founded United Artists.

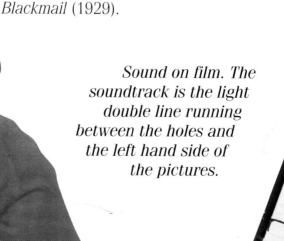

*Hitchcock's film* Blackmail *starred Donald Calthrop, John Longden and Anny Ondra.*

flood of would-be stars became so big that the local Los Angeles authorities begged them to stay away. They took no notice. There wasn't a waiter, a barman, a waitress or a cloakroom attendant for miles around who wasn't waiting for a passing movie mogul (the term the industry coined to describe its most powerful men) to 'spot' them and make them a star.

# THE COMING OF TALKIES

From 1900, it had been possible to show films and play sound at the same time. The words of the actors and the music were recorded on wax discs and played through a gramophone which was geared to run at the same speed as the film. But it was almost impossible to be absolutely sure that the sound came out at the right moment, and audiences used to howl with laughter when the female star was talking on screen while the male star's voice was ringing out from the gramophone.

What the industry needed was 'synchronised sound'. This means sound that is linked to the pictures and cannot fall out of step with the film. Synchronised sound came in 1923 when an American inventor, Lee de Forest, started making short films with the sound recorded on to the same strip of celluloid as the pictures. At one step, silent films became out-of-date – and so did some of the silent stars. A surprising number of silent movie stars came from non-English-speaking countries and some had very strong accents. Others had voices which came out high-pitched and squeaky on film.

The first 'talkie' was *The Jazz Singer* (1927) which starred singer Al Jolson. It was not entirely a talkie because although Jolson sang some songs and spoke a few lines of dialogue, the rest of the movie was silent. The first true all-sound 'talkie' was made the following year. It was a musical called *The Lights of New York*. At the same time, the British director, Alfred Hitchcock, made the first British 'talkie' – a film called *Blackmail* (1929).

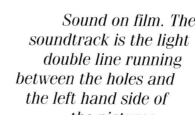

*Sound on film. The soundtrack is the light double line running between the holes and the left hand side of the pictures.*

# HOLLYWOOD AND THE STAR SYSTEM

In the ten years between 1920 and 1930, Hollywood became a teeming film town. The power rested with five major studios: Metro-Goldwyn-Mayer, Warner Brothers, Columbia, Paramount and 20th Century Fox. The studios themselves were like small towns divided up into areas called lots. Activity centred around the huge buildings in which the films were actually shot. These were known as sound stages, and the large studios had half a dozen of them in different sizes. All the other buildings, and the people in them, were there to serve the sound stages. Carpenters, costume-makers, make-up artists, script writers, administration personnel, sound engineers and film editors all worked to keep the sound stages busy. Outside shots were done in specially built sets on what was called the 'back lot'. Some studios used the same kind of set so often that these back lot sets became semi-permanent.

The studio heads were hugely powerful in Hollywood. None of them had actually been involved in making films before. Sam Goldwyn, for example, was a glove salesman from Minsk in Russia. These movie moguls kept careful control of their stars. Most Hollywood stars had contracts that tied them to work for their particular studio for seven years. The contracts looked generous to the young actors who hoped for success in Hollywood, but they were very one-sided. Stars were expected to live like stars and the studios encouraged them to buy fast cars and big houses with swimming pools and tennis courts – all of which cost a lot of money. If the film they were making was set in modern times, they were expected to provide their own clothes, although period costumes were provided by the studio. However,

**Curriculum Vitae:** Charlie Chaplin (1889-1977)

**Name:** Sir Charles Spencer Chaplin

**Place of birth:** London, England Charlie and his brother Sydney danced for pennies on the streets of London before being put in a home, from which Charlie escaped to join a dancing troupe at the age of eight. He and Sydney both joined the Fred Karno comedy company where Charlie was spotted on a tour of America by the boss of Keystone (see page 23). He made 35 films in his year with Keystone, earning £175 a week. Even after the arrival of talkies, *City Lights* (1931) made with only sound effects and music, was a huge success. He was a great believer in peace, and attacked both Hitler and the Nazi Party in his highly successful film, *The Great Dictator* (1940). He married Oona, daughter of playwright Eugene O'Neill, in 1943.

*An aerial shot of MGM Studios in 1940s. The studios covered 75 hectares and had six different lots. There were 30 sound stages on Lot 1 alone, employing over 5000 people.*

in every contract, there was what was called a 'suspension' clause. This meant that the star had to do exactly what the studio told them, or be suspended – laid off work without pay. The studios used this clause to force unwilling stars to make films, even if the star thought a particular film was unsuitable for his or her talents.

There were plenty of good things about the system, too. It looked after the stars from the time they got up in the morning to the time they went to bed at night. Women in particular were so protected that it was said that stars such as Elizabeth Taylor and Jean Simmons did not know how to do their own shopping or buy their own clothes. Like royal princesses of old, they were not required to handle money – it was all done for them.

## OUT TAKE

A few stars managed to break out of the studio system, one example being Humphrey Bogart who starred in many films including *Casablanca* (1941), *The Maltese Falcon* (1941) and *The African Queen* (1952). Bogart always put aside some of his pay cheques into a special fund he called his 'run off' money. When he was asked to do a film he thought unsuitable, he had money to live on while the row with the studio continued.

*A lifetime in the movies: Elizabeth Taylor at the age of 13 in* National Velvet *(1945) and in* Cleopatra *(1963)*

## OUT TAKE

Some male actors were quite small – but the film-going public liked its heroes to be larger than life. So camera trickery was used to make them look bigger. Alan Ladd was a star in Westerns of the 1940s and '50s. He was only 1.65 metres tall, which meant that he was often shorter than his leading ladies. When the script demanded that hero and heroine be seen together, the director used to provide a box for Ladd to stand on, or dig a hole for the actress to stand in.

*The Hollywood child star, Shirley Temple*

**Curriculum Vitae:** Louis B. Mayer of Metro-Goldwyn-Mayer (1885-1957)
**Name:** Eliezar Mayer
**Place of birth:** Minsk, Russia

Mayer emigrated to the USA with his parents as a child and grew up in his father's junk metal business. He bought one small run-down movie theatre in Haverhill, Massachusetts in 1907 and within seven years owned the largest chain of cinemas in New England. In 1918, he moved to Hollywood to make films, and in 1924 joined the newly formed MGM. He had a genius for matching the right star and the right film but he was loathed for his unfeeling treatment of his staff and stars. If he did not succeed by bullying, he would burst into tears to get his own way. On one occasion, he faked a heart attack to persuade an actress to sign up for a film she hated!

## THE SEARCH FOR QUALITY

In order to find good stories to feed the sound stages, studios maintained a system of scouts all over the world. The scouts looked out for books and stories that could be turned into a film idea. Famous writers such as the novelists William Faulkner and F. Scott Fitzgerald were hired to turn books into film scripts, known as 'screen plays'.

The cinema loved a good-looking child, too. Shirley Temple started by mimicking famous stars such as Marlene Dietrich in a series of short films called *Baby Burlesks* when she was only four years old. She was the star in *The Little Colonel* (1935) at the age of six. By 1938, aged ten, she was America's top box office attraction. A whole industry developed around her, with Shirley Temple dolls, colouring books and dresses.

## CENSORSHIP AND THE HAYS CODE

Many Hollywood stars became legends in their own lifetime. One great female star, Mae West, earned herself a name for her tough, funny, one-line wisecracks, many of which she wrote herself. However, her words turned out to be too sexy for

Hollywood. By 1922 there had been several scandals involving the motion picture industry, and movie-makers were already worried that their films might be censored by the government. To prevent this, the studios set up their own censorship office under a former lawyer called Will H. Hays. In 1934, Hays introduced the Motion Picture Production Code – a list of 'dos and don'ts' for people making films.

Under the Hays Code, strong language and swearing were strictly forbidden. Married couples were to be shown in twin beds, never sharing a double bed. As a result of the Hays Code, the final line of the film *Gone with the Wind* (1939), starring Clark Gable and Vivien Leigh, has become famous. The studio argued furiously that Gable should be allowed to say the line: "Frankly, my dear, I don't give a damn!" In the end, Gable was allowed to say the line, but only if he put the emphasis on a word other than 'damn'! Gable's delivery: "Frankly, my dear, I don't GIVE a damn!" has become a part of movie history. The Hays Code, which was widely disliked, survived until 1966.

# THE COMING OF COLOUR

The first films to appear in colour in 1896 were coloured by hand, requiring teams of artists wearing magnifying glasses to paint each inch-square frame. This was a massive job, because 1000 frames had to be painted for every minute of film. In 1905, a French movie-maker called Charles Pathé developed a process called Pathécolor, and in 1906 a British film-maker called George Albert Smith developed a new way of colouring film called Kinemacolor. At first, Kinemacolor used two colour filters, red-orange and blue-green. Like all movie film, the process depended on the phenomenon of 'persistence of vision' (see page 12). To use this natural trick of the eye, the Kinemacolor process filmed and projected a movie at 32 frames per second – twice the normal speed. By alternating the blue-green filter and the red-orange filter, it fooled the eye into thinking it saw colour. There were, however, many drawbacks to the system. It led to eye strain, and colour tended to 'drift' from one frame to the next.

The real breakthrough came in 1915, with the invention by Herbert Kalmus and Daniel Comstock of a system they called Technicolor. The first Technicolor system also used red-orange and blue-green filters, but it had two separate apertures both throwing the image on to the same film. An improved version came in 1932, when Technicolor produced a three-colour camera. This camera filmed through a single lens but the light was absorbed by three different negatives sensitive to the colours green, red and blue. The three-colour negatives were then

*A three-strip Technicolor camera dating from the 1930s*

*Judy Garland as Dorothy and Ray Bolger as the Scarecrow in* The Wizard of Oz, *one of the most famous of the three-colour Technicolor feature films.*

printed together on to a single positive, from which the final prints were made. The first film to benefit from this was a short movie made in 1933, but it was quickly followed by *Becky Sharp* in 1935. The most famous early colour films are *The Wizard of Oz* (1939) and *Gone with the Wind* (1939).

# THE WAR YEARS AND AFTER

The USA did not enter World War II (1939-45) until 1942, so the early war years were 'business as usual', although the film industry made it quite clear that it was opposed to fascism and the Nazis. Anti-war and anti-fascist films such as *Foreign Correspondent* (1940) sounded passionate warnings about the danger of the fighting in Europe. There were also plenty of films aimed at the entertainment market. Alfred Hitchcock made *Rebecca* (1940) with Joan Fontaine as a young wife trying to escape the evil influence of her husband's dead first wife. Humphrey Bogart starred in *The Maltese Falcon* (1941). Even *Casablanca* (1941), with Bogart, Claude Rains and Ingrid Bergman as three people

## OUT TAKE

The first cinemas were often converted music halls, but as movies became increasingly popular, more and more purpose-built cinemas were built. Some of these buildings were so grand that they became known as 'picture palaces'. Their lavish interiors were often modelled on famous foreign palaces or Egyptian temples, and known by such names as The Alhambra and The Ritz. The Roxy in New York was the largest in the world, seating 6214 people and employing a staff of 300 when it opened in 1927. The first purpose-built cinema in Britain was christened simply The Central Hall, and opened in Colne, Lancashire, on 22 February 1907.

caught up in Nazi-dominated French North Africa, was a story about personal relationships rather than a war story.

The years after the war brought new faces and names. Marilyn Monroe drove her fellow actors mad because she was incapable of remembering her lines or even turning up on time, but any film she was in sparkled like no other. In *Some Like it Hot* (1959), she played the sizzling star of a women's orchestra in the 1920s. Alfred Hitchcock, who started making films in the 1920s, also flowered in the 1950s. He made a series of thrillers including *Strangers on a Train* (1951), *Psycho* (1960) and *North by Northwest* (1959) in which Cary Grant is mistaken for an international spy and has to flee for his life. This film is unforgettable for two moments: when Grant is hounded through a cornfield by a crop-spraying plane, and the final scene on the sculpted heads of American presidents on Mount Rushmore.

*The German film-maker Leni Riefenstahl. One of her most striking films was* Olympia, *a record of the 'Nazi' Berlin Olympics in 1936.*

## OUT TAKE

During World War II, the Nazis used film to great effect. One of the most talented directors of the time was the German Leni Riefenstahl, a former ballet dancer, painter and actor. She was Hitler's favourite film-maker and was given the job of filming the Nazi Party Convention in Nuremberg in 1934. The resulting documentary, *Triumph of the Will*, is one of the most effective propaganda films of all time.

# 3 FILM GENRES

Films can be divided by subject matter or 'genre' (the French word for 'type' or 'kind'). Some studios and stars found that their talents were more suited to one kind of film than another. Warners, for example, were famous for their gangster movies during the 1930s. In Britain, the Ealing Studios built up a name for witty, very British comedy. Among modern stars, Bruce Willis has a face and physique more suited to tough, hard action than, for example, Woody Allen. In this chapter you will find some of the genres into which the industry divides its productions, as well as a few examples of each genre.

*A collection of Bonds: George Lazenby (top left), Roger Moore (top right), Sean Connery (bottom left) and Timothy Dalton (bottom right).*

## ACTION AND ADVENTURE

Action and adventure movies are fast and furious – and great fun to watch. The *Die Hard* movies in which Bruce Willis takes on a succession of smooth-talking evil geniuses with little more than his fists and his wit are a prime example of this genre. Other non-stop action films include *Independence Day* (1996), in which a lucky pilot and a computer expert defeat an alien invasion, Harrison Ford's *Air Force One* (1998) and *The Fugitive* (1993). An early action hero was *Tarzan*, played by a succession of athletic actors, but never better than by Johnny Weissmuller, a former Olympic swimmer.

## OUT TAKE

The James Bond films, based on the books of Ian Fleming, are in a genre of their own. Packed with action, they started with *Dr No* (1962), which made Sean Connery into an international star overnight. However, the more recent of the Bond films are not based on original Fleming stories. There have been several Bonds, including Roger Moore, George Lazenby, Timothy Dalton and, most recently, Pierce Brosnan.

Five more action and
adventure films to view:
*The Matrix* (1999) Director:
Andy and Larry Wachovski
Stars: Keanu Reeves, Laurence
Fishburne
*True Lies* (1994) Director:
James Cameron
Stars: Arnold Schwarzenegger,
Jamie Lee Curtis
*The African Queen* (1951)
Director: John Huston
Stars: Katharine Hepburn,
Humphrey Bogart
*The Charge of the Light
Brigade* (1936) Director:
Michael Curtiz
Stars: Errol Flynn, Olivia de
Havilland, David Niven
*The Thirty-Nine Steps* (1935)
Director: Alfred Hitchcock
Stars: Robert Donat, Madeleine
Carroll

*Covered in sweat and blood,
Bruce Willis saves the world
while hanging from a fire
hose over Los Angeles in
Die Hard (1988). The
formula was so successful
that it led to two sequels.*

*Mel Gibson and Lucy Alexis Liu meet in* Payback *(above), and Michael Caine surveys the loot in* The Italian Job *(below).*

# CRIMES AND CAPERS

Crime movies of all kinds have been the backbone of the cinema ever since it was invented. *The Great Train Robbery* (1903) made by Edwin S. Porter for Edison (see page 19), was both a crime movie and a Western, and the genre developed from there. In the 1930s, gangster movies starring people such as Edward G. Robinson and Humphrey Bogart were very popular. More recently, crime movies have become more bloody. Quentin Tarantino plunged into violent crime in films such as *Reservoir Dogs* (1991), and Mel Gibson took things even further with *Payback* (1999). Crime can also be funny. The 'Pink Panther' series features Peter Sellers as a bumbling, incompetent – and hilarious – French policeman. Crime 'caper' movies are often based on the careful planning of a master-crime which usually goes wrong in the last moments. One example is *The Italian Job* (1969) which stars Michael Caine and three fast-driven Mini Coopers!

Five more crime and caper films to view:
*The Silence of the Lambs* (1991) Director: Jonathan Demme
Stars: Anthony Hopkins, Jodie Foster
*GoodFellas* (1990) Director: Martin Scorsese
Stars: Robert de Niro, Ray Liotta, Joe Pesci
*Dirty Harry* (1971) Director: Don Siegel
Stars: Clint Eastwood, Harry Guardino
*The Godfather* (1972) Director: Francis Ford Coppola
Stars: Marlon Brando, Al Pacino, Diane Keaton
*Bonnie and Clyde* (1967) Director: Arthur Penn
Stars: Warren Beatty, Faye Dunaway

# COMEDY

Comedy has been a winning genre ever since the early days of films and the Lumière brothers' *L'Arroseur Arrosé* (*The Waterer Watered* 1895) (see page 17). The silent era specialised in comedy, with famous names such as Charlie Chaplin, and Laurel and Hardy. After the introduction of sound, one team with universal appeal was the Marx Brothers. More recently, Roberto Benigni wrote, directed and starred in *La Vita e Bella* (1997) which won three Oscars in 1999. It is a story about a man who tries to protect his son from the horrors of a Nazi concentration camp by convincing him that it is all a game – and it manages to be funny. A darkly comic movie is *Trainspotting* (1996) about a drug addict. More wacky humour is found in *Wayne's World* (1992) featuring Mike Myers and Dana Carvey as the presenters of a cable TV show.

Five more comedies to view:
*Crocodile Dundee* (1986) Director: Peter Faiman
Stars: Paul Hogan, Linda Koslowski
*Annie Hall* (1977) Director: Woody Allen.
Stars: Woody Allen, Diane Keaton
*Monty Python and the Holy Grail* (1975)
Director: Terry Gilliam
Stars: Graham Chapman, John Cleese,
Terry Gilliam
*A Funny Thing Happened On The Way
to The Forum* (1966)
Director: Richard Lester
Stars: Zero Mostel, Phil Silvers,
Michael Hordern
*Kind Hearts And Coronets* (1949)
Director: Robert Hamer
Stars: Dennis Price, Sir Alec Guinness,
Valerie Hobson

Crocodile Dundee *made Paul Hogan
into an international star while*
Wayne's World *(inset) created
a new genre of
youth comedy.*

# DISASTER MOVIES

The disaster movie is an enduring favourite. Burning buildings, crashing aeroplanes, sinking boats and natural disasters like earthquakes or volcanic eruptions are all guaranteed to keep movie audiences on the edges of their seats. Historical disasters such as *Krakatoa East of Java* (1968), about an island volcano which blew up in 1883, and *The Last Days of Pompeii* (1935) about another famous volcanic eruption in Roman times, were both great successes. But the most successful film of all time in financial terms is the disaster movie *Titanic* (1998). The action showing the world's worst peacetime sea disaster was skilfully executed, using a replica ship only 32 metres shorter than the real thing and a film crew of 800.

**Five more disaster films to view:**
*Deep Impact* (1998) Director: Mimi Lederer
Stars: Robert Duvall, Vanessa Redgrave, Morgan Freeman
*Meteor* (1979) Director: Ronald Neame
Stars: George C. Scott, Anne Bancroft
*The Hindenburg* (1975)
Director: Robert Wise.
Stars: Sean Connery, Natalie Wood, Karl Malden
*The Towering Inferno* (1974)
Director: John Guillermin
Stars: Paul Newman, Steve McQueen, Faye Dunaway
*A Night To Remember* (1958)
Director: Roy Baker
Stars: Kenneth More, Honor Blackman, David McCallum
*San Francisco* (1936)
Director: W. S. Van Dyke
Stars: Clark Gable, Spencer Tracy

*A Boeing 707 jet engine was used to create the tornadoes in the Michael Crichton film* Twister *(1996), starring Helen Hunt and Bill Paxton as tornado hunters.*

# HISTORY AND COSTUME

Films set in past times, often known as costume dramas, have a natural attraction for movie-makers. Ancient Rome was so full of colour and action that it became a familiar background. *Quo Vadis* (1912) (see page 20) was unrivalled for spectacle until Charlton Heston took the reins of his chariot in *Ben Hur* (1959). Robin Hood may not have existed in real life, but he provides ideal subject matter for the film industry. He has been portrayed on screen at least 52 times, most recently by Kevin Costner in *Robin Hood, Prince of Thieves* (1991) and Patrick Bergin in *Robin Hood* (1991). (Mel Brooks sent them both up in his comedy version, *Robin Hood – Men In Tights* (1993). But the classic version is Errol Flynn in *The Adventures of Robin Hood* (1938) with its sword fight on the stairway, often seen only in the fantastic shadow play of the combatants on the wall.

Five more costume dramas to view:
*The Madness of King George* (1994)
Director: Nicholas Hytner
Stars: Nigel Hawthorne, Helen Mirren
*A Room with a View* (1986)
Director: Ismail Merchant
Stars: Helena Bonham-Carter, Daniel Day-Lewis
*The Fall of the Roman Empire* (1964) Director: Anthony Mann
Stars: Alec Guinness, Christopher Plummer, Stephen Boyd
*Captain Horatio Hornblower, RN* (1951) Director: Raoul Walsh
Stars: Gregory Peck, Virginia Mayo, Robert Beatty, James Robertson Justice
*The Three Musketeers* (1948)
Director: George Sidney
Stars: Gene Kelly, Lana Turner, Van Heflin, Vincent Price

*Robin Hood (Errol Flynn) and Sir Guy of Gisbourne (Basil Rathbone) cross swords in their classic screen duel at the climax of* The Adventures of Robin Hood *(1938). It has always been held to be the best* Robin Hood *ever made.*

## OUT TAKE

William Shakespeare is in a class of his own in movie-land. He is the most filmed writer ever. There are more than 275 'straight' versions of his plays, and at least 25 'modernised' stories based on the plays. One of the most recent, *Shakespeare in Love* (1999), was written by Tom Stoppard and picked up no fewer than seven Oscars. Dame Judi Dench (left), who won an Oscar for Best Supporting Actress, said that she was amazed to win because she was on screen for only eight minutes during the whole film!

## OUT TAKE

The fictional character most portrayed on screen is Sherlock Holmes, the great detective created by Sir Arthur Conan Doyle. There have been 175 films, many featuring Basil Rathbone (right) who played the great detective in a series of films made in the 1940s. The real-life historical character to appear most frequently on screen is the French emperor, Napoleon Bonaparte. He has been portrayed in at least 163 films since 1897, not least by Marlon Brando (*Desirée* 1954) and Rod Steiger (*Waterloo* 1970).

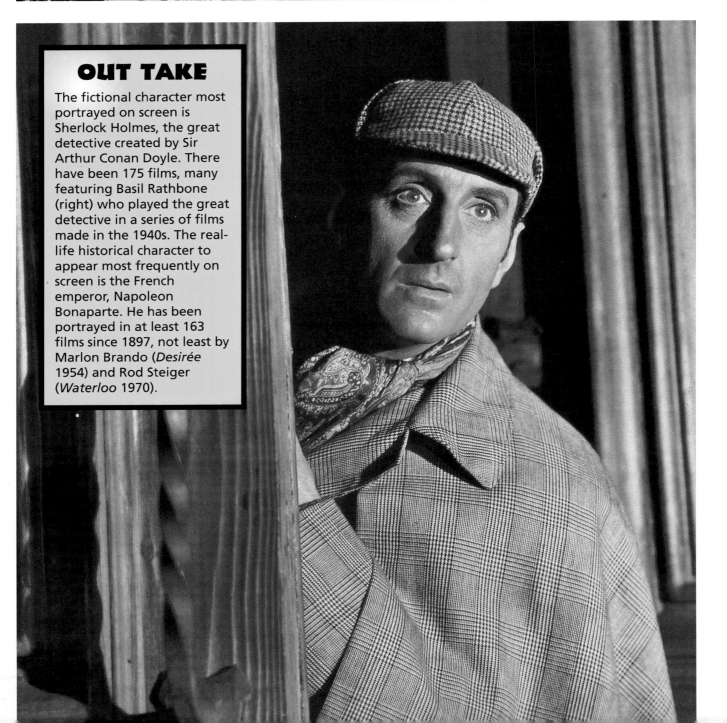

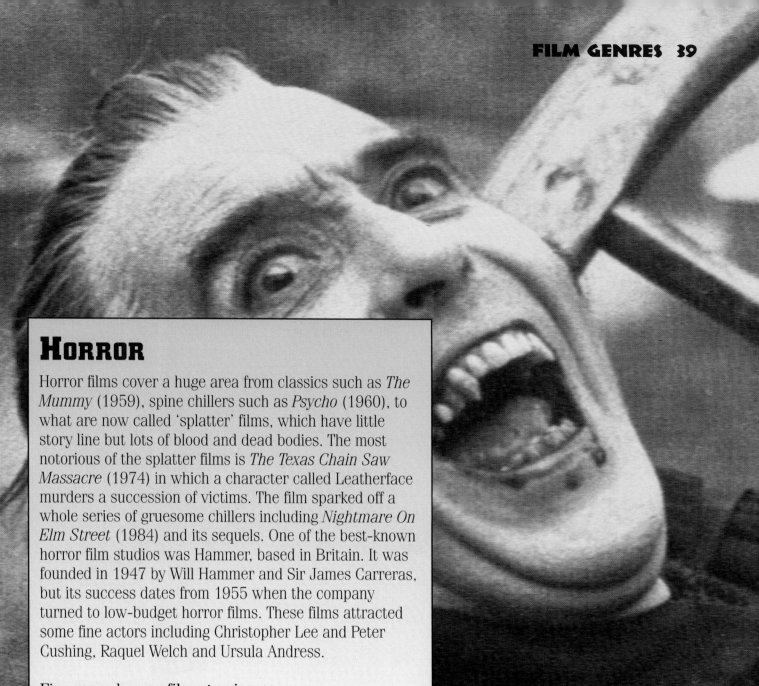

# Horror

Horror films cover a huge area from classics such as *The Mummy* (1959), spine chillers such as *Psycho* (1960), to what are now called 'splatter' films, which have little story line but lots of blood and dead bodies. The most notorious of the splatter films is *The Texas Chain Saw Massacre* (1974) in which a character called Leatherface murders a succession of victims. The film sparked off a whole series of gruesome chillers including *Nightmare On Elm Street* (1984) and its sequels. One of the best-known horror film studios was Hammer, based in Britain. It was founded in 1947 by Will Hammer and Sir James Carreras, but its success dates from 1955 when the company turned to low-budget horror films. These films attracted some fine actors including Christopher Lee and Peter Cushing, Raquel Welch and Ursula Andress.

Five more horror films to view:
*Mary Shelley's Frankenstein* (1994) Director and star: Kenneth Branagh
Stars: Robert de Niro, Helena Bonham-Carter
*An American Werewolf in London* (1981)
Director: John Landis
Stars: David Naughton, Jenny Agutter
*Alien* (1979) Director: Ridley Scott
Stars: Sigourney Weaver, John Hurt, Ian Holm
*Jaws* (1975) Director: Steven Spielberg
Stars: Robert Shaw, Roy Scheider
*Nosferatu* (1921) Director: F. W. Murnau
Star: Max Schreck

*Christopher Lee as Dracula in 1972*

## MUSICALS

Musicals delighted cinema audiences, and it is no coincidence that the first talkies were musicals. Busby Berkeley's films were packed with dozens of dancing girls in spectacular dance routines. *Gold Diggers of 1935* (1935), *For Me and My Gal* (1942), and dozens of others left audiences spellbound. *Seven Brides for Seven Brothers* (1954) was wonderfully colourful and spectacular. It was made to try and entice dwindling audiences away from the new attraction of television and back into the cinemas. *The Sound of Music* (1965), with Julie Andrews as a singing nun in Nazi-occupied Austria, is probably the most enduring musical hit. Recent years have seen film musicals such as *Evita* (1996), which starred Madonna as the tragic wife of the dictator of Argentina.

Five more musicals to view:
*Grease* (1978) Director: Randal Kleiser
Stars: John Travolta, Olivia Newton-John
*My Fair Lady* (1963) Director: George Kukor
Stars: Rex Harrison, Audrey Hepburn
*West Side Story* (1961) Directors: Robert Wise, Jerome Robbins
Stars: Natalie Wood, Russ Tamblyn
*Singin' In the Rain* (1952) Director and choreographer:
Gene Kelly
Stars: Gene Kelly, Donald O'Connor, Debbie Reynolds
*The Wizard of Oz* (1939) Director: Todd Holland
Stars: Judy Garland, Frank Morgan

*George Chakiris in a street-gang dance in* West Side Story.

# SCIENCE FICTION

Films set in space, on far-flung planets or in the distant future have always attracted the movie-makers. The earliest movie in this genre, *Voyage dans la Lune* (*A Journey to the Moon* 1902), was made by the pioneer Georges Méliès (see page 18). Since then science-fiction ('sci-fi' for short) films have been made about time travel, lost worlds, all sorts of rockets and spaceships, robots and androids. Special effects are very important in these films, for example Stanley Kubrick's *2001: A Space Odyssey* (1968) used model space ships to great effect. Science fiction is often uncannily accurate in the things it predicts will happen in the future. Experiments to use a super-gun to shoot satellites into space are remarkably similar to Méliès' astronauts in *Voyage dans la Lune*. Epic series such as the 'Star Wars' and the 'Star Trek' films are classic examples of the sci-fi genre.

Five more science-fiction films to view:
*Blade Runner* (1982)
Director: Ridley Scott
Stars: Harrison Ford, Rutger Hauer
*E.T.* (1982) Director: Steven Spielberg
Stars: Dee Wallace, Henry Thomas
*The Abyss* (1973)
Director: James Cameron
Stars: Ed Harris, Mary Elizabeth Mastrantonio
*Westworld* (1973)
Director: Michael Crichton
Stars: Yul Brynner, Richard Benjamin.
*Metropolis* (1926) Director: Fritz Lang
Stars: Brigitte Helm, Alfred Abel

*Captain Jean-Luc Picard (Patrick Stewart) sorts out the rebels in* Star Trek: Insurrection *(1998).*

*Clint Eastwood as the 'man with no name' (in* For a Few Dollars More*)*

*Monument Valley, Utah, USA, became the location for many Westerns, including* Stagecoach.

# THE WILD WEST

Probably the most prolific of the film genres is Westerns. The first Western-set film was made by The Edison Company in 1894. It was actually a series of short films called *Sioux Indian Ghost Dance*, *Indian War Council*, and *Buffalo Dance*. The first Western star was G. M. 'Broncho Billy' Anderson, who made 400 Broncho Billy films before 1918, when competition from other actors forced him out of the business. The greatest of the Western stars was John Wayne. Born Marion Morrison in 1907, and known to his friends as 'the Duke', Wayne had his first starring role in *The Big Trail* (1930), and over the next eight years made over 80 low-budget Westerns. It was Ford who cast him as the Ringo Kid in *Stagecoach* (1939), considered to be one of the best Westerns of all time. Wayne became the biggest draw the cinema has ever seen. Westerns became such a dominant genre that whole series of them were made outside the USA. The best and most famous are the 'Spaghetti Westerns' made by Italian companies at locations in Spain, and pioneered by Italian producer Sergio Leone with the 'Man with No Name' trilogy. The 'man with no name' was played by Clint Eastwood who went on to make many other films as a tight-jawed, slit-eyed tough guy.

Five more Westerns to view:
*Dances with Wolves* (1990) Director: Kevin Costner
Star: Kevin Costner
*Once upon a Time in the West* (1969) Director: Sergio Leone
Stars: Henry Fonda, Claudia Cardinale, Charles Bronson
*A Fistful of Dollars* (1964) Director: Sergio Leone.
Stars: Clint Eastwood, Gian Maria Volonte. (Sequels: *For a Few Dollars More* (1965) and *The Good the Bad and the Ugly* (1966))
*The Magnificent Seven* (1960) Director: John Sturges.
Stars: Yul Brynner, Steve McQueen.
*The Searchers* (1956) Director: John Ford
Stars: John Wayne, Jeffrey Hunter, Natalie Wood

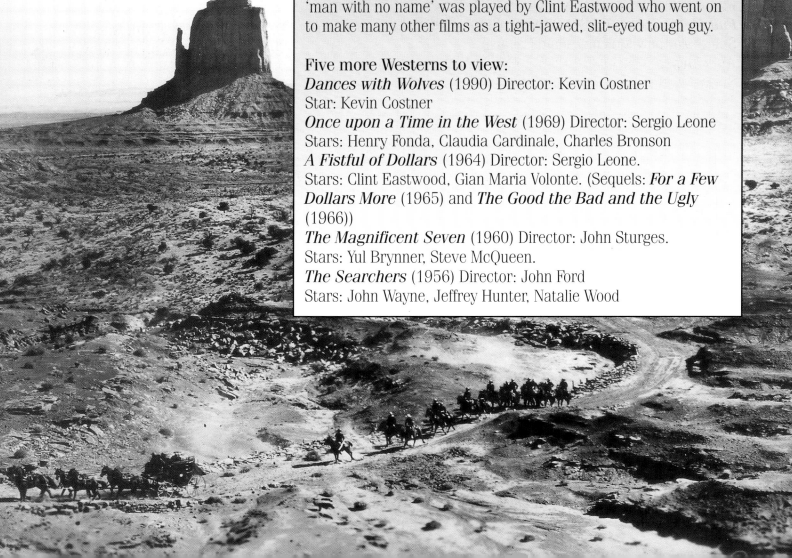

# GOING TO WAR

Many war films have a strong underlying anti-war message, even when they are great action stories on the surface. *All Quiet on the Western Front* (1930) was a German story about the futility of the trench warfare in World War I. *Paths of Glory* (1957) starred Kirk Douglas in a story of three French soldiers condemned to die for cowardice in the same war, but was a savage attack on the corruption and incompetence of their commanders. Of course, views of war change. *In Which We Serve* (1942) was made in the darkest days of World War II, and starred Noel Coward in an unashamedly patriotic story about the wartime navy. *The Cruel Sea* (1953) showed German U-boats and their crews as evil threats, whereas *Das Boot* (*The Boat* 1981) showed those same German U-boat crews as heroic men daring all for their country. Similarly, the films *Saving Private Ryan* (1998) and *The Longest Day* (1962) take very different looks at the invasion of Normandy in 1944.

Five more war films to view:
*Full Metal Jacket* (1987) Director: Stanley Kubrick
Stars: Matthew Modine, Adam Baldwin
*Apocalypse Now* (1979) Director: Francis Coppola
Stars: Martin Sheen, Robert Duvall
*M.A.S.H.* (1970) Director: Robert Altman
Stars: Donald Sutherland, Elliott Gould
*The Dirty Dozen*(1967) Director:
Robert Aldrich
Stars: Lee Marvin, Telly Savalas, Donald Sutherland
*The Bridge on the River Kwai*
(1957) Director: David Lean
Stars: Alec Guinness,
William Holden

## OUT TAKE

In 1910, Charles Pathé launched the modern form of news coverage, stringing together several unrelated items in a package to make a news feature or 'newsreel' which was shown at cinemas. Soon there were special small cinemas called News Theatres which ran continuous hour-long programmes of newsreels and cartoons. They were often placed close to train or bus stations where travellers with a short time to wait could pay a small sum to sit and be informed and entertained. However, the start of television news in the 1950s spelled the end of news in the cinema.

*A scene from the Francis Coppola film* Apocalypse Now

*Hugh Grant starred in the hugely successful* Four Weddings and a Funeral.

# 4 DIFFERENT COUNTRIES: DIFFERENT CINEMA

People often refer to film-land as 'Hollywood' whether they mean America or not, so it has become a shorthand way of describing the whole cinema industry. In fact, there are thriving studios all over the world which have little to do with the west coast of America.

## BRITAIN

From the earliest days, the British film industry has turned out excellent films. Alfred Hitchcock, the master of suspense (see page 31), did his early work in Britain, although he regularly commuted to Hollywood before finally going to live in the USA. British cinema has always had a character of its own, and nowhere is this more clearly shown than in its comedy. In the 1940s, Michael Balcon at Ealing Studios launched a series of films which were characteristically British. Among these were witty comedies such as *Kind Hearts and Coronets* (1949) in which Alec Guinness plays no fewer than eight roles in the story of a young man killing his way to a title. Other comedies such as *Whisky Galore!* (1949), about a Scottish island that benefits when a ship full of rare whisky is wrecked on its shores, were notable because they showed a downtrodden group rebelling against authority.

Other important figures in the British film industry include Alexander Korda and David Lean. Hungarian-born Alexander Korda was the director and producer of films such as *The Private Life of Henry VIII* (1933), *The Third Man* (1949) and *Richard III* (1956). David Lean joined Gaumont as a clapper boy (see page 75) in 1927 and went on to make such movies as *In Which We Serve* (1942) a very effective war propaganda film, and *Brief Encounter* (1945) a study in controlled passion between Celia Johnson and Trevor Howard. Later he made epics such as *The Bridge on the River Kwai* (1957), *Lawrence of Arabia* (1962) and *Dr Zhivago* (1965) with equal success.

## OUT TAKE

Hollywood got its name from a large ranch which originally stood on the site of the film studios. The huge sign on the hill overlooking Los Angeles was erected in 1923 at a cost of $21,000 and it used to read: HOLLYWOODLAND. The letters are made of sheet metal and each one is nine metres wide and 15 metres tall. At one time the sign was studded with lightbulbs and a man called Albert Kothe was employed full time to change the ones that burned out. He lived in a hut behind one of the 'L's.

# HOLLYWOOD

**Curriculum Vitae:**
Charles Laughton (1899-1962)
**Born:** Scarborough, England
Laughton started life as a hotel clerk but opted for the stage after World War I. He won an Oscar for his portrayal of the much-married king in *The Private Life of Henry VIII* (1933) in which he starred with his wife, Elsa Lanchester. Then he went to Hollywood and made *Mutiny on the Bounty* (1935) with Clark Gable as mutineer Fletcher Christian. In 1950 he became an American citizen. In his many movies, he starred as servant and statesman, as an American lawyer and even as Quasimodo in *The Hunchback of Notre Dame* (1939) – but he never failed to dominate the screen.

The British film industry has often had unexpected successes with movies made on small budgets and from unexpected sources. *Four Weddings and a Funeral* (1994), starring Andie McDowell and Hugh Grant, was the most successful British film of all time to date, and set a style followed up in *Notting Hill* (1999). Directors such as Mike Leigh, Derek Jarman and Peter Greenaway have all been responsible for innovative and award-winning films.

# RUSSIA

In Russia, the potential of cinema for use as propaganda was recognised almost as soon as movies started to appear. After the Russian Revolution in 1917, the Russian leader, Lenin, said: "For us, the cinema is the most important of the arts." He sent out trains which were fitted as travelling cinemas to move around Russia and take the message of the new Communist government to the masses. The 'agit-prop' (the term comes from the words 'agitation' and 'propaganda') films shown on these trains were made by teams from Moscow to get across the message of the Communist party. In a country where there were more than 100 different languages, silent film and its universal vocabulary were useful tools. The directors of these agit-prop films developed some clever techniques for filling the screen, such as cutting between subjects and people with great speed to communicate both urgency and enthusiasm. This technique developed to become known as 'montage'.

From the 1920s, Russian cinema was dominated by the work of Sergei Eisenstein, a former cartoonist one of whose early jobs was decorating the agit-prop trains. Eisenstein is known particularly for the films *Strike* (1924) and *Battleship Potemkin* (1925) the true story of the mutiny of sailors on a battleship in Odessa. The film is famous for scenes such as the one on the Odessa steps which shows innocent civilians being shot down by soldiers. Eisenstein did not believe in single central characters, and he used masses of people moving from place to place with dramatic effect. *Alexander Nevsky* (1938), the story of a historic Russian hero, and the epic *Ivan the Terrible* (1945) are among Eisenstein's other masterpieces.

During the era of Communism, Soviet film-makers had to work under the strict regulation of the government – yet despite persecution from the authorities, directors such as Andrei Tarkovsky continued to make films of great inventiveness. It was not until the 1980s that films-makers in Russia could work without interference from the government (see page 79).

*An agonised mother mourns her murdered child in the famous Odessa steps sequence from Eisenstein's* Battleship Potemkin.

*Marlene Dietrich plays a nightclub dancer in* The Blue Angel, *a film of which she later said: "I was shocked by the whole thing!"*

## OUT TAKE

It was in Italy that the first epics were made (see page 20), and Italian cinema always excelled at opulent costume epics – particularly of classical tales. After a period of repression during World War II, the Italian film industry came back to life with a series of films that gave rise to the term 'neorealism'. This was a technique of using realistic, gritty locations to take an unflinching and vivid look at post-war life. It started with Lucino Visconti's *Ossessione* (1942) and was used in Roberto Rossellini's *Rome, Open City* (1945), a tale of the Italian underground movement in Rome. Neorealism came to maturity in Federico Fellini's *La Dolce Vita* (1960) in which a young tabloid reporter comes to realise the shallow and worthless lives of the society figures of Rome, yet is unable to change himself.

# GERMANY

German cinema started before the turn of the century. In fact, a few weeks before the Lumière brothers were showing their cinema films in Paris, two German brothers called Max and Emil Sklandanowski were displaying moving pictures to a paying audience in Berlin. After World War I, German cinema began to experiment with the grotesque in films such as *The Cabinet of Dr Caligari* (1919) directed by Robert Weine. What became known as 'expressionism' used distorted sets and deliberately unnatural lighting to make movies look macabre.

In the 1930s Germany was in the grip of a strict political regime – that of the Nazis. With a few exceptions such as *The Blue Angel* (1930) starring Marlene Dietrich, and the thriller *M* (1931), the German film scene was dominated by political propaganda films. Those made by Leni Riefenstahl, (see page 31) are remarkable films, even if they do show the Nazis in a very flattering light. After the end of the war, the German film industry made movies for the home market until a group of young film-makers banded together in 1962 to establish New German Cinema. The best-known international figures to come out of this movement were the directors Rainer Werner Fassbinder, Wim Wenders and Werner Hertzog.

*Anita Ekberg on the poster for* La Dolce Vita, *a film that revealed the life of the rich and idle in Rome*

FEDERICO FELLINI'S **LA DOLCE VITA** Starring Marcello Mastroianni Anita Ekberg Anouk Aimee

*A poster for* Mon Oncle. *The film is a comedy in which a young boy becomes more fond of his bumbling uncle than his parents.*

# FRANCE

**Curriculum Vitae:** Jeanne Moreau (b.1928)
**Born:** Paris, France
Moreau became famous for her participation in the French New Wave, both as actor and director. She acted in her first film in 1949 (*Le Dernier Amour, The Last Love*), and soon became the world-weary face of the New Wave in films such as *Moderato Cantabile* (1960) and *Jules et Jim* (1961). In the 1970s she directed *La Lumière* (*The Light* 1976) and *L'Adolescente* (*The Adolescent* 1978).

The art of cinema was born in France (see page 17), and French cinema has always been full of challenging and exciting ideas. Among the finest French film-makers was Jean Renoir, son of artist Pierre Auguste Renoir. Jean Renoir's *The Rules of the Game* (1939) showed up the corruption at the heart of the French establishment and was thought to be so dangerous that for a while it was banned. When it was shown the film was fiercely cut by the film censor (see page 79), and it was not seen in its original, uncut version until 1965. There is classic humour in the films of Jacques Tati, who starred as the pipe-smoking M. Hulot in a series of light-hearted comedies including *Jour de Fête* (1949), *M. Hulot's Holiday* (1953) and *Mon Oncle* (1958).

In the 1950s, a group of young directors rebelled against what they saw as slick and predictable cinema in France and in Hollywood. They formed a movement which came to be known as 'La Nouvelle Vague' (New Wave). These film-makers created intensely personal films in which they expressed their own individuality. The best-known examples of this movement are *Hiroshima, Mon Amour* (1959) directed by Alain Resnais, and Jean-Luc Godard's *A Bout de Souffle* (*Breathless* 1959). Another influential New Wave film-maker was François Truffaut. His *Les Quatre Cent Coups* (*The Four Hundred Blows* 1959) about a 12-year-old boy who finds himself in a detention centre, escapes – and just carries on running – was said to be based on his own early life.

# JAPAN

For many years Japanese cinema, though producing plenty of films, remained a home-based industry. Then, in 1950, the film *Rashomon* took the top prize at the Venice Film Festival, and went on in the following year to show the richness and imagination of the Japanese industry to the rest of the world. It was made by Akira Kurosawa.

Some Japanese films have been used as the basis for successful Western stories. For example, *Seven Samurai* (1954) about a group of warriors hired to protect a village from bandits was made into the popular Western, *The Magnificent Seven* (1960) starring Yul Brynner, in which Mexican villagers do exactly the same thing with a group of gunfighters.

**Curriculum Vitae:** Akira Kurosawa (1910-98)
**Born:** Tokyo, Japan
Trained as a painter, a talent he used to make the storyboards for his films, Kurosawa started in the Japanese film industry as an assistant director in 1936 and went on to direct his own films. *Drunken Angel* (1948) was the first film to feature Toshiro Mifune who became a star and appeared in most of Kurosawa's subsequent movies, including *Rashomon* (1950). *Rashomon* made Kurosawa's name internationally, and *Seven Samurai* (1954) confirmed this reputation. He was also known for his reworkings of Western classics including *The Throne of Blood* (1957), an adaptation of Shakespeare's *Macbeth*, and *Ran* (*Chaos* 1985), based on Shakespeare's *King Lear*.

*Toshiro Mifune (left) in* Rashomon

# AUSTRALIA

The first feature film was produced in Australia in 1906. It was *The Story of the Kelly Gang* about a gang of criminals made famous when their leader, Ned Kelly, tried to escape a police ambush in a home-made suit of sheet metal armour. The film even boasted that it used the real Ned Kelly armour. During the period before World War II, Australia was mainly known for the quality of its documentary films, and many won awards. More recently, films such as *Picnic at Hanging Rock* (1975), *Crocodile Dundee* (1986) and *Strictly Ballroom* (1992) have delighted people all over the world. The 'Mad Max' series of films, with their inventive and brutal picture of life after some unspecified disaster in the future, brought Mel Gibson to the notice of an astonished world.

*Holly Hunter and Anna Paquin both won an Oscar for* The Piano

## OUT TAKE

Although it may be a small area, Hong Kong is a dynamic one. Hundreds of films have been produced there but in the 1970s, karate and kung fu combat films became the speciality. The American-Chinese actor Bruce Lee was the best-known star of these films. Lee made a series of films including *Fists of Fury* (1972) and *Enter the Dragon* (1973) before his mysterious death at the age of 32.

*Bruce Lee's all-action, super-fit kung fu hero sparked off a whole series of imitations.*

# BOLLYWOOD

The most successful film-making industry outside Hollywood is in India. Centred on Bombay, which is known as 'Bollywood', the Indian film industry makes between 700 and 800 films a year – more than twice the number made in Hollywood.

Film came to India in 1896, when the Lumière brothers showed six short silent films at the Watson's Hotel in Bombay. Within a short time, two producers, Hiralal Sen in Calcutta and H. S. Bhatavdekar in Bombay, were making films and, in 1899, Bhatavdekar was already showing his own factual, silent films in Bombay. India is a subcontinent with a huge variety of languages, so when the first feature film, *Raja Harishchandra*, came out in 1913 it carried subtitles in both Hindi and English.

By 1927, the Indian industry was making 27 features a year and, by the time the first Indian talkie was issued in 1931, that number had risen to 207. *Alam Ara*, the first talkie was also the first musical. A singer called W. M. Khan performed on the soundtrack, starting the

Indian tradition of the movie song, which survives to this day. Other traditions that became firmly established included romantic musicals, with strong love stories and choreographed violence, and mythological drama, rooted in ancient Indian folklore.

The director, Satyajit Ray, took the next giant step when he directed the film *Pather Panchali* (1955). The film went on to win an award at Cannes the following year, picked up a nomination for best film at the British Academy awards in 1958, and has not stopped winning awards since. This was the film that brought the Indian film industry to the attention of the rest of the world. Since then, the Indian film scene has gone on developing. Amitabh Bachchan, a superstar of the Indian film industry, developed a series of roles in which he created the angry young Indian who stands up to authority. His film, *Sholay* (1975) was the biggest-earning of all time until it was overtaken in 1995 by the blockbuster *Hum Aapke Hain Kaun*, starring Madhuri Dixit.

The Indian film industry deals in enormous figures. Over the century, it has produced more than 27,000 films in 52 languages, not counting factual and documentary films, made countless stars, and established big production centres all over the subcontinent, including cities such as Calcutta, Madras and Lahore. Indian films are exported all over the world and shown to enormous audiences.

*Indian cinema often draws heavily on legend and fable, and is lavishly and colourfully produced.*

Pather Panchali *is about a young boy growing up in a poor family in Bengal.*

# 5 ANIMATION

Walt Disney once said: "The duty of cartoons is not to duplicate but to give a caricature of life and action." The principle of using a series of drawn images to create the illusion of movement is old. It was used in the optical toys and machines of the 19th century (see page 13), for example the Praxinoscope. In the late 1880s the inventor of the Praxinoscope, a Frenchman called Emile Reynaud, went on to develop the Théâtre Optique. He painted pictures on to glass slides by hand, mounted them on a leather strap, and cranked the strap through the machine by hand. He showed his 15-minute slide shows with great success in Paris in the 1890s and later used celluloid film, but he could never keep up with the demand, and he went out of business.

In 1908, another Frenchman called Emile Cohl made the first 'modern' cartoon, drawing each frame by hand, and photographing the drawings frame by frame. The cartoon was two minutes long and called *Fantasmagorie*. The following year, a film of a character called Gertie the Dinosaur appeared, drawn by Winsor McCay. McCay was an artist who worked for the newspaper the *New York Herald*. He had a music-hall act, and he introduced Gertie to the public as part of his act, projecting the cartoons on to a screen on stage, talking to Gertie and getting her to do tricks. His finale was when he walked off stage and re-appeared as a small figure in his own cartoon!

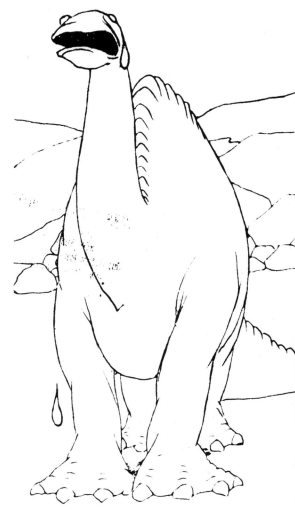

*Gertie the Dinosaur as drawn by her creator, Winsor McCay*

## THE COMING OF CELS

Both Cohl and McCay drew their cartoon characters by hand on to paper and then filmed them frame by frame. However, the cartoons appeared to 'flicker' as they were shown. This was a result of the movement from one drawing to the next, and it was quite noticeable. Other cartoonists began to work on ways to get rid of the flicker. In 1914 there was a breakthrough by Earl Hurd. Hurd invented what became known as the 'cel' – a sheet of transparent celluloid.

In each frame of a cartoon there is a part of the picture that does not change, and a part of it that does. In a cartoon sequence of a running person, for example, the body can stay still while the legs run along. The static part of the picture is drawn on one sheet of celluloid. The moving part – the legs – is drawn on to a second, a third and a fourth cel, each taking the movement a stage

*An artist paints an image on a cel. The gloves protect the cel from dirty fingermarks.*

further. The second cel is laid over the first and the combination is photographed. It is then replaced by the third cel, on which the legs are a little further into the movement, and that combination is photographed and so on until the required movement has been finished. Since the camera is photographing the same basic shapes, there is no 'flicker' as the cartoon moves forward. And instead of the painstaking process of re-drawing the whole picture each time the artist wants to introduce movement, all the cartoonist has to do is replace the elements of the picture that are required to move. This method eliminated the flicker of the paper-based drawings. By adding extra cels, the animation can be made more and more complicated. So successful is the cel method that it is used to this day.

The art of the cartoon spread quickly. Gertie the Dinosaur was joined by all kinds of other moving creatures and, by 1920, the most popular of the silent cartoon characters was Felix the Cat, brought out by Otto Messmer and Pat Sullivan. At the same time, another promising young cartoonist was learning his trade. His name was Walt Disney and, in the 1920s, he was already becoming known for his high-quality work and carefully written scripts.

With his lifelong collaborator, Ub Iwerks, Disney set up his own studios and brought out the first of his animal characters: Oswald the Rabbit. The first two stories featuring Mickey Mouse, *Plane Crazy* (1928) and *Gallopin' Gaucho* (1928), were both silent. But Disney immediately saw the value of sound, and Mickey was heard to speak for the first time in *Steamboat Willie* (1928). Disney did the squeaky voice himself.

*Walt Disney's easy-going smile masked an iron will. Disney was a hard boss as well as an animation genius.*

**Curriculum Vitae:** Walt Disney (1901-66)
**Place of birth:** Chicago, USA
Disney trained as an artist but at the age of 16 volunteered as a Red Cross ambulance driver, and spent the last months of World War I in France. On his return to the USA in 1919, he went into cartoon animation where he met a man called Ub Iwerks, and a winning partnership was formed. Together, they went to Hollywood in 1923, where they produced a series of cartoons called 'Alice in Cartoonland'. In 1927 they invented the 'Oswald the Rabbit' series and, in 1928, Mickey Mouse. After World War II, the company branched out into feature films with live actors. The first was *Treasure Island* (1950), a great success. In 1955 Disney opened the first Disneyland in Anaheim, California. During his life, he won 29 Oscars for his films, including the highly successful 'True Life Adventure' series which started with *Seal Island* (1949) and included *The Living Desert* (1953) and *Jungle Cat* (1960).

# THE COMING OF COLOUR

It was natural that cartoonists should want colour as well as sound for their films. The first colour cartoon was hand painted on celluloid (see page 16) and then photographed using Brewstercolor. It was a silent film called *The Debut of Thomas Kat* and it appeared in 1920. In 1932, Disney came out with the colour and sound film *Flowers and Trees.* It was the first cartoon to be made with the three-colour Technicolor process (see page 29). However, it was Dave and Max Fleischer, the creators of the Popeye and Betty Boop characters, who were Disney's main competitors. The two studios raced against one another to bring out the first feature-length cartoon, and Disney won with *Snow White and the Seven Dwarfs* (1937). It took 200 animators three years to bring the 82-minute film to the screen and it required more than two million drawings. In 1940, Disney issued *Pinocchio*, followed by *Dumbo* (1941) and *Bambi* (1942).

By the 1930s, Walt Disney was the most powerful man in the cartoon business, but at the peak of his achievement there was a growing unease even among his own artists that he was too big and too successful. The pressure on his vast organisation to keep up the output was thought by some people to be taking away the freshness and originality of his cartoons. Several cartoonists split off from the Disney studios and set up their own production company, United Productions of America (UPA). They created characters such as Mr Magoo and McBoingBoing. At the same time, Warners had their own cartoon section which included Tex Avery, Chuck Jones and Fritz Freleng. They created such characters as Bugs Bunny, Daffy Duck and Wile E. Coyote and the Roadrunner. To this day, Bugs' catch phrase is: "Eh, what's up, doc?" because Avery came from Texas where 'doc' was a nickname, just like 'mate'.

*Daffy Duck is a cheery, funny character*

# MAKING CARTOONS

*Rough sketches are drawn to plan the progress of the storyline, creating a storyboard. Each storyboard page usually has six frames.*

In some animation studios, cartoons are made by the traditional method, using cels (see pages 51-2). In others, computers have replaced some of the most time-consuming processes.

First, the story line is discussed and laid out. Once the characters are decided, the artists draw them in various forms until the editor chooses the final versions. These then become the permanent characters, and all artists have to draw them in the same way. The story is sketched out in a series of pictures, called the 'storyboard'.

The next step is to write the script and record the soundtrack. The director times each sound on the soundtrack and works out how many frames of action will be needed to match it. This information is recorded on to the 'dope sheet'. The dope sheet is passed out to the artists who are going to draw the actual cartoons, so that each knows exactly how much action he or she needs to provide and in how many frames.

The background to each scene is fixed and painted on to a paper background by one artist. Then the cels (transparent acetate sheets) are drawn by a team of artists. The cels are laid over the background and fixed exactly in place with a line of pegs, so that they cannot shift in relation to the base sheet. The base cel contains the static part of the picture. The other cels contain the elements of the drawing that are required to move. When the cels are ready, they are mounted on an animation board under a rostrum camera. The camera points straight down on to the picture and it can move up and down, to produce long shots and zoom. Each exposure is

*The layout artist draws the background to a scene. This background (below) will be scanned into the computer for the characters to be added later.*

*The director and animator works on the character of a dog. Note the 'dope sheet' next to him, guiding his work, which must fit exactly into the time allotted to the dialogue.*

made following the instructions of the animator who is responsible for the cartoon, and recorded on the exposure sheet to make sure that the pictures follow one another in exact sequence.

The cartoonist has to draw 24 separate drawings for every second of screen time, which means that a 10-minute cartoon needs more than 14,000 drawings. In studios such as London-based Telemagination, hand-painted cels, which can take days to paint and dry, have been replaced by a computer program. Hand-made drawings are scanned into the the computer, as well as a 'colour model' telling the computer which colours to use. This process starts with the background on which the stories will be based, then the individual characters are scanned in. The computer is told in which order to place the images. Finally, the characters are coloured and combined with the pre-drawn background. Work which would take many people several days when hand-painting on to individual cels now takes a matter of hours on a computer. And if changes are needed, the computer can be adjusted without the hugely expensive process of remaking the cels.

*The digital artist colours in a character on the computer screen, according to a previously scanned 'colour model', and places it against the scanned background.*

When the pictures have been photographed or created on the computer, they must be combined with the soundtrack, which may be recorded on as many as 12 different reels. Music, sound effects and dialogue must be carefully synchronised with the pictures so that they come at exactly the right moment. All the sound is mixed on to a single soundtrack. The soundtrack and the colour negatives of the animated story are then sent off together to the laboratory for the combined track and animation prints to be turned into a film ready for the cinema. There is also usually a video tape of the cartoon for broadcast on television.

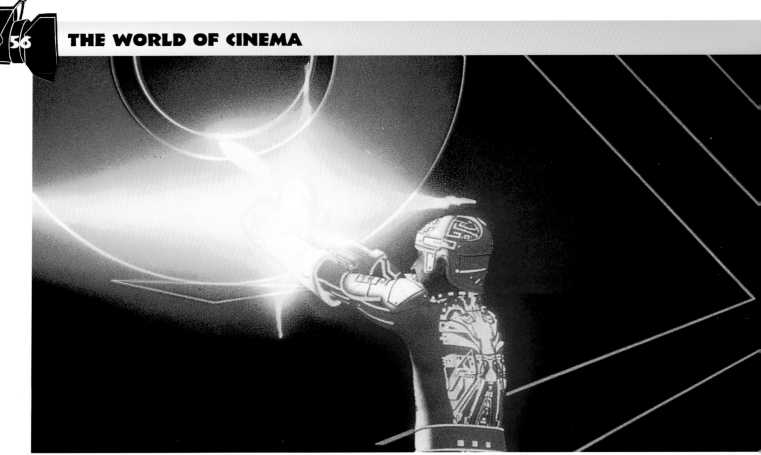

Tron *was the first film to combine computer action and human actors. Bruce Boxleitner starred as a computer games designer forced to fight his enemy within the computer.*

## COMPUTERS

One problem with cartoon films is that they are very labour-intensive. It takes hundreds of artists months to produce animated drawings. However, by feeding the same information into a computer and telling it to animate the characters, a lot of repetitious work can be cut out.

Using computer software, it is also possible to make films which combine live actors and cartoon characters. The first feature film to benefit from this technology was made by Disney – and it was set inside a computer. *Tron* (1982) was an action adventure film that combined real actors with computer-generated special effects. The story, which starred Bruce Boxleitner, was about a computer games designer who got his revenge on an enemy by fighting it out inside a computer game he had himself designed. It was not long before the Disney team used computers to produce a full-length feature film. *Beauty and the Beast* (1991) was made in the style of a Broadway musical and won an Oscar for its music soundtrack. It was a combination of traditional cartoon animation and computer-generated scenes.

Computer animation opened the doors to all kinds of cinema wizardry, including the special effects generated for *Terminator 2* (1991), in which Arnold Schwarzenegger fought with a version of a robot made from liquid metal. The process by which human or human-like characters are put into a computer's memory is called

### OUT TAKE

One technique that uses computers to create dramatic special effects is called 'morphing'. This is when a real life image is merged with another image created by the computer. It was first used in *Willow* (1988) but really came into its own to transform Jim Carrey from a wimpish bank clerk into a green-faced cartoon super-hero in *The Mask* (1994).

A Bug's Life *from Pixar Animation Studios used* Toy Story *techniques to tell the story of a rebel ant who recruits a circus troupe to fight off grasshoppers who prey on his community.*

Antz *deliberately made its on-screen characters look human.*

'motion capture'. Sensors are put on to an actor's face and body and linked to a computer which records the movements and the actions of the actor's face and body in its memory.

Once the computer has recorded what happens when a human being walks, runs, sits down and stands up, it can reproduce these actions again and again. This is called 'performance animation'. It was used at the Pixar Animation Studios in California by 26 animators working on over 100 computers to bring out the successful film, *Toy Story* (1995). This movie was the first completely computer-animated feature film. Since then *Antz* (1998) and *A Bug's Life* (1998) have also been hugely popular.

# 6 SPECIAL EFFECTS

One of the aspects of film-making that calls for the most ingenuity is special effects, known for short as 'SFX'. In many ways, there is not much difference between the magical tricks of Georges Méliès (see page 18) and the high-tech world of *Titanic* (1998). Both are designed to make the audience think that they see reality when in fact they see only illusion. Méliès learned his first SFX trick, stop-action photography, by accident. One day his camera stuck in the middle of filming a street scene in Paris, and by the time he got it going again the scene he was filming had changed. He wrote in 1907: 'Projecting the film, having joined the break, I suddenly saw a Madeleine-Bastille omnibus changed into a hearse and men into women.' Animators have used the same trick ever since – though the methods have been improved over time.

Computers, which made such a difference in the making of cartoons (see pages 56-7), have also revolutionised SFX. Hit films such as *Jurassic Park* (1993) and *Titanic* owe a great deal of their success to the use of computer-generated or computer-enhanced special effects. The SFX in these films are a combination of something happening in front of the camera and something being improved (or 'enhanced') by technology behind it.

## OUT TAKE

In *Titanic*, computer animation was used to people the decks of the doomed ship with passengers. There are, however, some drawbacks to using computer animation and live actors in the same scene. The actors cannot see computer-generated scenery, characters or creatures and some find it difficult to act around a space which will later be filled by a computer-generated image. In scenes where a crowd of real people all need to look at the same invisible computer-generated image, for example a monster, it is often difficult to get everyone looking at the right spot, and it is easy to end up with the crowd staring metres above the monster's head in the finished shot.

## MAKING THEM MOVE

One way of making monsters and fictional creatures move, apart from building a big model or putting an actor into a body suit (see pages 61-2), is to use stop-action. This works in much the same way as cartooning with cels (see pages 51-2). The animator makes a model from some flexible material, based on a metal framework, and takes a picture of it. Then he or she moves the limbs a tiny amount and takes a second frame. Frame by frame, the action builds up until the animator has a whole sequence.

One of the first people to use this method on a feature film was the American film-maker Willis O'Brien, who made *King Kong* (1933) and its sequels. O'Brien started by making clay models of his figures, but he soon found that the clay became deformed each time he moved the figures, meaning that he had to keep re-modelling them. So O'Brien made his monsters from latex which he cast into the required shapes and mounted on a pliable metal skeleton called an 'armature'. *King Kong* used several models 45 centimetres high, and one 5.5-metre model for close-ups.

It combined the animated model of Kong with live actors such as Fay Wray who was picked up and cuddled like a kitten by the devoted Kong. Kong ended up climbing the Empire State Building in New York and batting at fighter planes as though they were irritating mosquitoes.

Nick Park of Aardman Productions uses Plasticine to model his characters. In the Oscar-winning film, *Creature Comforts* (1989), Park put the words of everyday conversations into the mouths of zoo animals made from Plasticine. *Creature Comforts* and the later films, *The Wrong Trousers* (1993) and *A Close Shave* (1995), were all filmed in sets less than a metre high.

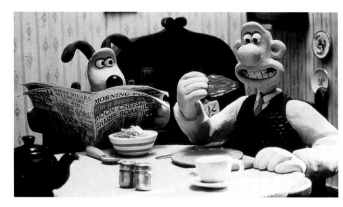

*Wallace and Gromit, the stars of Nick Park's* The Wrong Trousers

**Curriculum Vitae:** Willis O'Brien (1886-1962)
**Born:** Oakland, California
O'Brien was a cartoonist and commercial sculptor whose work was exhibited at the San Francisco World Fair in 1913. He was fascinated by the new world of movies and started experimenting with special effects in short films the following year, before going on to feature films in the 1920s. He made a series of feature films, including *The Last Days of Pompeii* (1935), *The Black Scorpion* (1957) and *The Lost World* (two versions, in 1925 and in 1960). But his greatest creation was *King Kong* (1933), and its sequels *Son of Kong* (1933) and *Mighty Joe Young* (1949). In the new version of *Mighty Joe Young* (1999) the massive ape, Joe, is played both by an actor in a body suit and a computer-generated image.

*King Kong takes on the US Air Force*

*Max Schreck with enlarged ears and central fangs in* Nosferatu

# MONSTER MOVIES

One of the most exciting types of film is the monster movie. Movie monsters are safe monsters because we leave them behind in the cinema when we go home. Of course, this does not mean that the monsters are any less frightening on the screen!

The first screen monster to make a real impact on a cinema audience was a German actor, Max Schreck. He shaved his head and wore fangs and graveyard eye make-up to play the first screen vampire in silent film *Nosferatu* (1922). Schreck wore his vampire teeth in the middle, as opposed to the now traditional fangs worn at the side by other famous vampires such as Christopher Lee – the most successful Dracula of them all (see page 39). A more recent portrayal was *Bram Stoker's Dracula* (1992), which starred Gary Oldman and Winona Ryder.

*Pinhead was the monster created for* Hellraiser *(1987) and was used on the poster for the film.*

*Monster-maker Martin Astles crops the ears of a latex demon's head mask.*

# MONSTER-MAKERS

One of the most experienced monster-makers is Bob Keen who runs Image FX Animation in the UK. Keen and his team of artists, sculptors, electronic experts and computer-operators have made more than 1000 monsters for over 100 films, including Jabba the Hutt for the 'Star Wars' film *Return of the Jedi* (1983). At 5.5 metres long Jabba was the biggest monster Keen has ever built. This monster was very complex because it had to perform all kinds of actions, and it was far too big to be a 'body suit' monster – in which an operator performs the movements from inside. So the monster contained small electric motors called 'servos' in its face which could be operated by remote controllers – just as model aircraft are controlled. The mouth was operated manually by a puppeteer. For the 1999 prequel (a film in the same series but set earlier in time than the original), *The Phantom Menace*, Jabba was recreated by computer.

*Jabba the Hutt interviews Han Solo in the 1997 edition of* Return of the Jedi.

Body-suit monsters look basically human because they are occupied by a human operator. The Alien in *Alien* (1979) and the alien monster in the Leslie Nielsen film, *2001, A Space Travesty* (2000) are both body-suit monsters. Body suits are built up in layers. First, the muscles are sewn or moulded individually on to a Lycra all-over garment. Over the top of the 'muscle suit' goes an

**OUT TAKE**

'Animatronics' is the technique of operating inanimate objects to make them look as though they are actually alive. These techniques were developed by both the Jim Henson Creature Shop, which produced *The Muppets*, and the Disney organisation, to operate the larger-than-life-size figures of Mickey Mouse and his friends for their theme parks.

outer skin, also mounted on a Lycra backing, which can be painted and made up. If the creature is truly alien, the monster-makers cast a foam latex outer skin on to the Lycra base while it is stretched over a human form. Once the latex has dried and set, the body suit is cut to insert concealed zips.

The actor inside the body suit is too busy acting like an alien to manipulate the features of the head and any other special effects 'extras' (such as antennae or extra limbs). So these areas are operated by remote control. The shape of the face is made from a metal and fibreglass skeleton with a foam-rubber moulded skin over the top of it. In this skeleton an animatronic engineer fixes servos (electric motors) which will animate the muscles of the face, move the mouth and eyes, and raise and lower eyebrows. It takes surprisingly few servos to provide a range of expressions. The servos are operated by a puppeteer using a radio control box. The movements of the face are recorded by a computer which can then duplicate the same movements over and over again as required. Ten years ago, a monster required up to ten puppeteers to control the different parts of its body and face. Now, one puppeteer can work the creature through a programme of movements, which are fed into the computer. The combination of actor inside the suit and the puppeteer and computer outside it makes the monster perform as required.

**OUT TAKE**

Some actors dislike body suits because they are hot, airless and uncomfortable. It is very hard to see out, and if the actor's eyes can be seen, it means he or she has to wear 'full eye' contact lenses. Once they are in the suit, it is difficult for actors to sit, eat or drink without the whole make-up being redone.

*Roddy McDowall has to hold his mask mouth open to get his lunch into the real thing during the shooting of* Planet of the Apes *(1968).*

# The 'BOO moment'

The people who make monster movies know that it is not necessarily the monster itself that frightens people but the suspense in the film. So movie-makers use all kinds of tricks to heighten the suspense.

Lightning is a well-known trick – it means that the audience won't see all the monster at once. Corridors are useful because the monster can be glimpsed a long way away. Seeing something slither away in the gloom is better than a full view because your own imagination invents all kinds of horrors. Sometimes the monster in your mind is far worse than the one on screen. Seeing the whole of the shark in *Jaws* (1975), for example, is almost an anticlimax after the shock of seeing the fisherman's severed head fall out of his boat.

The monster in *Alien*, on the other hand, lives up to expectations, possibly because it is both armoured and slimy at the same time. Even so, you actually see the whole monster only at the end of the film. Until then, it is just a series of horrifying snatches of detail. In the sequels, although there are several monsters, they somehow lose their impact.

Movie-makers have special names for the moments that really frighten the audience in a film. There is the 'scare moment' when the audience gets its first sight of a bit of the monster. Then there is the 'grab factor' which makes the audience jump because someone was suddenly grabbed. But the most important one is the 'BOO moment'. This is when the audience sees a monster up close for the first time. It can make or break a monster movie, because if it does not live up to expectations, suspense will be replaced by laughter. If the 'BOO moment' makes the audience laugh, the film is a failure.

*The 'BOO moment'! Bruce the Great White shark opens wide in* Jaws.

## OUT TAKE

A film does not even have to contain a visible monster to be frightening. One of the most effective ghost movies ever made was *The Haunting* (1953). It starred Richard Johnson and Claire Bloom as ghost hunters investigating a haunted house. Doors bulge, lights dim, something fumbles its way along the corridors in the dark, handles move by themselves – but the audience never actually sees a ghost at all.

# STUNTS, FIRES AND EXPLOSIONS

Fire and flames are almost impossible to fake, and very dangerous to work with. Actors are rarely risked in explosions and fires. Usually, their place is taken by expert and tough stunt men and women, who also perform other dangerous tasks such as falling down stairs, diving off buildings and climbing steep surfaces.

For scenes that feature fire, stunt men and women use specialised equipment to prevent them being burned. The stunt person wears fireproof underwear soaked in protective gel, and covered with a flameproof suit. The face is covered with a hood which is in turn covered by a fire mask moulded to look like a face. Life-like moulded gloves protect the hands. If a fall is included, the stunt person wears body armour and padding. Over the protective gear goes a specially made version of the star's costume. The scene is filmed from an angle that does not show the face clearly, or from far enough away for the face to be indistinct.

A full-scale fire need not always actually consume the building in which it is filmed. Inflammable gel can be spread along brick walls and ignited to provide real flames which will eventually go out of their own accord. Gushes of controllable flame can be provided by gas jets which can be turned down or even off when they are not being filmed. Safety is paramount in all special effects, of course, but nowhere is it more important than in fire scenes. There are always professionals standing by with water and extinguishers to step in if things become too realistic for comfort.

*In this fire stunt a stuntman covers his 'face' with his 'hands' – fireproof gloves – to prevent his face mask being seen.*

*Catherine Zeta Jones crosses swords with Antonio Banderas in the fencing scene from* The Mask of Zorro.

# FIGHTS AND BULLETS

All fights are dangerous, even when they are faked. Fight arranging is an art, and the people who can do it are highly prized. The most dangerous are sword fights, because even a blunt sword is a dangerous strip of metal which can easily maim or kill. Sword fight arrangers rehearse the fighters carefully, and most screen fencing matches are as choreographed as a ballet dance. Each fighter has to know exactly where his or her opponent will be at every moment. Catherine Zeta Jones, for example, had two tasks in her spectacular duels with Antonio Banderas in *The Mask of Zorro* (1998). She had to avoid scarring her co-star and she had to avoid being marked herself. This is not just natural human concern for the actors' well being – it would be very expensive to halt filming while the star recovers from an injury!

Bullet wounds are created by putting small capsules of blood-red paint into a 'squib'. This is a very small explosive charge that is fired electronically. Another method is to fire soft gelatin capsules from a specially made compressed air gun. The capsules splash on impact, giving a realistic bullet wound.

# WORKING MODELS

When large pieces of equipment are needed for a movie, such as historic ships and planes, a producer can either hire them from one of the several specialist companies around the world, build them, or use models. Sometimes, a combination of all three methods is used. If a company has spent $2million on a reconstructed 18th-century frigate, it is not going to sink it in a simulated sea battle or allow it to burn. So specialist model-makers produce a smaller replica. The normal scale is one-sixth real size. But the difficulty of model work is to make the model look right in its environment. If the waves of the 'sea' – in fact a massive tank – look wrong, even the best model in the world will not be convincing.

For the film *Interview With The Vampire* (1994), it took four people two months to create the waterfront of the Bay of Naples from 446 square metres of plywood, for a scene in which the vampire's ship arrives. The shot on screen lasted seconds. When a 17th-century galleon was supposed to burn and sink in a storm for *Cut Throat Island* (1995), two full-sized galleons were built in Malta as well as a 15-metre replica for sinking purposes in the studios.

*Bandits attack the floating island in Kevin Costner's hugely expensive film* Waterworld.

However, expense does not always guarantee success. When Kevin Costner made *Waterworld* (1995) he is said to have spent $175 million, making this seaborn epic the most expensive film ever. Most of it went on constructing a floating island. It did make money at the box office, but nothing like the profits Costner might have expected from a real hit.

# FLYING

Early films used invisible wires to make people 'fly'. An actor wore a harness similar to a parachute harness under his or her costume, and was hooked up to a crane and lifted into the air. The trouble was that the clothes (or, in the case of Batman or Superman, his cloak) remained limp because the actor could not be moved fast enough to create a draught. More recently, a television technique called 'chromakey' has been developed. In this method, the actor is filmed against a plain blue background, and the clothing and hair is blown around by a wind machine to simulate flying through the air. The background against which the actor is to be seen 'flying' is filmed with another camera, and the two are combined in a machine called an optical printer. The optical printer can combine several different effects and bring them all together at once.

*The shadows and the umbrellas give it away, as comedian Ben Turpin clowns in fur for a comedy snow scene at the Sennet studios in Los Angeles in the 1920s. The icicles were painted cut-outs and the 'snow' was made from soap and salt.*

# WEATHER

Nobody can rely on the weather to fit in with the script, so film producers have to be ready to provide their own. Wind is produced by large wind machines, based on aeroplane engines. Rain can be switched on to order with specially built rain machines like huge garden sprinklers when the action takes place out of doors, or through a sprinkler system hanging from the studio roof when in a sound stage. Snow is generated through a fan system and these days is made up of powdered polystyrene which is light enough to 'float' down and does not dissolve as soon as it hits the ground.

One part of almost all film 'weather' is stage smoke. This is produced by pouring a vegetable-based oil into a hot element in a smoke machine, and it can be used to simulate mist, provide the slightly 'foggy' atmosphere to dim outlines in heavy rain or snow, or simply to provide smoke for fire scenes. Almost all battle scenes on film contain smoke in one form or another, to convey the confusion and uncertainty of a real battlefield.

# 7 MAKING A MOVIE

Making a movie is a complicated and painstaking process. It involves a variety of talents, some highly technical know-how, and money – because film making is usually hugely expensive. For example, the budget for *Titanic* (1998) was $200 million, and for the 'Star Wars' prequel *The Phantom Menace* (1999) it was $110 million.

The whole process of making a film can be roughly broken down into four stages: development, pre-production, production and post-production.

*Sometimes, a gun just isn't enough: when Ripley (Sigourney Weaver) is forced to return to the breeding place of the monsters in* Aliens, *second in the successful series, she finds herself using powerful mining machinery against the horrors.*

# DEVELOPMENT

The producer is the most important person in the birth of any film. Producers take charge of the story, raise the money, select the director and the stars, and control the budget.

The first thing a producer needs is a 'property'. This is the story on which the film will be based. Agents all over the world seek out new stories and submit them to producers. Some films are based on ideas that have already been successful, as a stage play (*Dangerous Liaisons* 1988), as a book (*Trainspotting* 1996), or as a TV series (*The Fugitive* 1993). Some are made from an original idea, such as the Arthurian romp, *First Knight* (1995). If the producer

## OUT TAKE

Films are often sold on a very short description, known as 'the pitch'. The most famous of these was the pitch for the science-fiction film *Alien* (1979). It consisted of just three words: 'Jaws in space.' It was the perfect pitch because it described exactly what kind of film it would be, the fact that it would contain a monster, and the fact that it would thrill the audience.

**Curriculum Vitae:** Steven Spielberg (b. 1947)
**Born:** Connecticut, USA
Spielberg was making home movies almost as soon as he could walk. At the age of 12 he made his first scripted film with actors. At 13, he won a contest with a movie called *Escape to Nowhere*. He moved on to make TV films, including the terrifying *Duel* (1972) about a motorist on a state highway at night who finds himself in a motoring war with an anonymous truck driver. Spielberg has been responsible for a succession of hits including *Jaws* (1975), *Raiders of the Lost Ark* (1981), *E.T.* (1982), *Jurassic Park* (1993) and *Saving Private Ryan* (1998).

likes the story, the next step is to call in a scriptwriter. Between them they work out the 'treatment' – the outline of the film which they use to raise money. Not all properties actually make it to the screen, but the treatment is the first step in that direction.

Finding funds is the producer's next concern. This is done by persuading distributors, the companies that rent out films to cinemas, to lend the first instalment of the money needed to set up production. In return they are promised a share of the profits. The rest of the cash is raised from overseas distributors, banks or other investors. Once the funding is in place, the first person the producer needs is a director. This is the person who will actually make the film. Some producers are also directors, scriptwriters, and even actors. Quentin Tarantino, for example, combines all three roles in many of his movies.

*Director Steven Spielberg holds just two of the more than 30 major awards he has won so far in a lifetime of film-making.*

# PRE-PRODUCTION

Casting, finding locations, hiring props and studios, costume design and making scenery are all part of the process of pre-production. This is also the time to start pre-publicity (see page 80).

## CASTING

The producer and the director often work together to decide on the main casting for the film, but the practicalities are sorted out by a casting director. Choosing the right person for the role is a specialised art. Good casting directors know which faces, talents and physiques will suit a part. Sean Connery is wonderful as James Bond, Indiana Jones's dad, and the Captain of a Russian submarine (in *The Hunt For Red October 1990*), but would he make such a convincing bewildered time-traveller as Michael J. Fox in *Back to the Future* (1985) or as good a Scarlet Pimpernel as Richard E. Grant (1998)?

The casting director also organises the hiring of 'extras' – the non-speaking people in a film – and stunt doubles. Directors cannot risk a big star being hurt in a stunt, so a trained stunt person of similar build and colouring is hired to fill in for the star in dangerous scenes.

### OUT TAKE

Quite apart from their performances, top stars make huge contributions to the style of a film. When making *Saving Private Ryan* (1998) producer-director Steven Spielberg and star Tom Hanks were determined to make the epic as realistic as possible. Hanks insisted on wearing an authentic 27-kilogram pack, containing war-time rations of canned meat, cheese, crackers and chewing gum. Spielberg hired men who had lost legs or arms so that they could be fitted with artificial limbs which were 'blown off' during the film version of the invasion assault on Omaha Beach.

*The film* Gandhi, *directed by Richard Attenborough, used over 300,000 extras for some of its epic scenes.*

*Tom Hanks insisted on gritty realism for the Oscar-winning* Saving Private Ryan.

**OUT TAKE**

Movie-makers do not always have to build a real castle, or film on a real set to get the right scenery. Scenery is often provided by a 'matte'. In the matte process, the scenery is painted on to a sheet of glass, leaving a space for the action. The camera shoots through the glass, picking up the actors in the space.

*Oversized scenery was used to put this unfortunate boy in a bowl of cereal for the Disney film,* Honey, I Shrunk the Kids.

**OUT TAKE**

The scenery in the background of a film shot is not always real. The scenery can be projected on to a screen from behind, and the actors placed in front of the screen to play their scenes. This is called a 'process shot'. Scenes in which people are apparently driving cars through busy cities, for example, are often made with a process shot because it is much cheaper than taking actor, car and film crew out, stopping the traffic, mounting the camera on a truck and filming it live.

# SET DESIGN

A set is the area in which a film is actually made, including the scenery, props and surroundings. It can either be in a sound stage or on a location somewhere outside the studios. A location can be an existing structure, such as a castle or a suitable building, or a special piece of scenery built for the film, or open countryside – *Robin Hood, Prince of Thieves* (1991) was shot partly at the medieval city of Carcassonne in southern France and partly on Hadrian's Wall in northern England.

For *Shakespeare in Love* (1999), the director required a reconstruction of Elizabethan London, as well as a series of imposing palaces, castles and banqueting halls. To build a version of Elizabethan London, production designer Martin Childs made drawings and then models of the complete set before the construction work could start. The set was built in a market garden behind Shepperton Studios near London. It was a massive task that took a team of 115 people eight weeks. The set had 17 buildings including two theatres, a bawdy house, a tavern, a market place and Shakespeare's London garret. But for Viola's (Gwyneth Paltrow) home scenes, the filming moved to a different location at Broughton Castle in Oxfordshire. Old Greenwich Palace was played by Hatfield House, in Hertfordshire, and the banqueting hall in Whitehall by the Great Hall of the Inner Temple, in London.

Set design can also help with special effects. For monster movies, set designers often make miniature buildings. In 'shrinking person' films such as *Honey, I Shrunk the Kids* (1989) special giant sets and unnaturally large creatures were made. In the 'standing' or semi-permanent sets which were used time and time again at the Hollywood studios, buildings were made two thirds life-size. This made them cheaper to build, easier to maintain – and it also made the actors look bigger.

# THE DIRECTOR

The director is in charge of the creative work on the set. First of all, he or she must plan the 'shoot', working out which actors are needed when and where. Scenes must be shot in the most economical order so that actors can get all their work out of the way in the shortest possible time, both to suit their own schedules and to make sure that expensive stars do not spend days sitting around doing nothing. The director also has to make sure that locations are used economically and to the best effect.

On set, the director arranges the action in front of the camera, and controls the acting and the dialogue spoken by the actors. When the director, the scriptwriter and the producer have discussed the development of the story, the treatment is given to the screenwriters for them to produce the screenplay. The screenplay is the script from which the film will be made, and it is rewritten and changed many times before it actually gets to the actors. In a theatre, the script is usually followed closely. However, film scripts are subject to almost daily change, and it is not uncommon for actors to be presented with re-written scripts the night before for a scene they have already learned to perfection.

The script from which the director and cast actually work on set is called the shooting script, and it includes lighting and camera directions. These instructions are worked out between the director and the director of photography (also known as the lighting cameraman or the cinematographer). Such things as scenery, camera angles and lighting are very important, because the meaning of the scene may depend on what the audience can see in the background as much as on what the characters are actually saying. In *Jaws* (1975), for example, the line: "We're going to need a bigger boat" delivered by Roy Scheider to Robert Shaw during the shark hunt, only has full impact if you can see that in the background a huge shark has just emerged from the sea, unnoticed by Shaw.

*Alfred Hitchcock was one of the most important and influential directors of his time.*

# COSTUME

Actors say that, next to the script, the most important element in creating a character is the costume. Some actors even insist on invisible elements of costume being correct. When Lee Strasberg appeared in *The Godfather Part II* (1974), for example, he always made sure that his socks matched his suit – even though they never appeared on screen.

When actors put a costume on, they assume the character of the role they are playing. Particular movements and postures are

*Last-minute adjustments on the set of* My Fair Lady, *filmed in 1964. The lavish costumes were designed by Cecil Beaton who won an Oscar for his work – one of the seven Oscars awarded to the film.*

often imposed by costume – people walk differently in trainers from the way they walk in high-heeled boots. An Ancient Roman soldier wearing sandals does not march in the same way as a modern soldier in military boots. For the same reasons, actors have to learn how to move in period costumes. Victorian women wore crinolines – skirts supported by a series of hoops underneath. Instead of striding out, Victorian women took short steps to avoid stepping on the front of the skirt, and this is what modern-day actors have to learn to do. Men in period dress have different problems. Old fabrics crumpled easily, so a man in a coat with tails held his coat-tails out of the way to avoid sitting on them. Men also have to manage elaborate hats and swords.

Great care is spent getting the details of historical costumes right. For accuracy in close-up shots, machine stitching is regarded as far too neat, and seams and lapels are often sewn in deliberately visible hand-stitching. When the same piece of clothing appears in different states at different times in a film, several versions are made. A suit which is supposed to show the wear and tear of a journey through the jungle, for example, is deliberately 'sweat' stained with glycerine and make-up to age it.

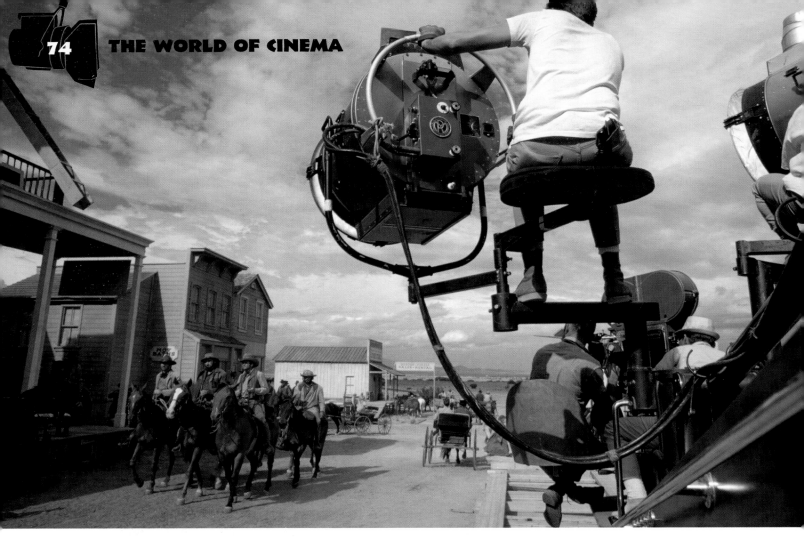

*"Action!" Filming a scene on location in Santa Fe, New Mexico, USA, for* The Cheyenne Social Club *(1967) which starred Henry Fonda and James Stewart.*

# PRODUCTION

Once the film is in the studio, it is shot by the camera operator, who works the camera. He or she is assisted by the focus puller (or first assistant cameraman), whose job it is to change film and filters, look after the camera and the exposed film, keep a log of which shots are in which cans and when they were taken, and measure the distance between the lens and the actors by pulling out a tape measure which is built into the camera. Since correct focus is absolutely crucial to the quality of the film, nothing is left to chance. The positions in which the actors are required to stand during a scene, or from which they are expected to deliver their lines, are marked on the floor with T-shapes of sticky tape or chalk. 'Hitting your mark' without looking at it is one of the basic skills required of an actor.

The mark is also crucial to the sound recordist. He or she places the microphone at the end of a counter-balanced, extending arm called the sound boom. This holds the mike out of shot but close to the actor's head. The sound recordist starts the scene by making sure there is no sound coming through the microphone which is not required by the script – for example the sound of a passing airplane – and then shouting "Sound running!" and then "Clear!" to allow filming to start.

*Nicholas Cage is about to get into a rough scene once the clapper board has been snapped down to start this take from* Con Air *(1997).*

The camera operator is also in charge of the clapper loader (or second assistant cameraman), who is responsible for the clapper board. This is a slate on which is written the name of the film, the number of the scene and the number of the take. Attached to the top is a wooden strip which is hinged at one end. This strip is snapped down to make a sharp sound which is used later when the film is edited to synchronise the soundtrack and the pictures. Once the director is sure that all is well with the camera and sound, he or she shouts "Action!" to give the actors the signal to start the scene. To stop the action, the director shouts "Cut!"

## OUT TAKE

The members of a film crew are called by some odd names:

**Art director:** the person responsible for everything the camera sees – from the scenery and outdoor settings to the properties that fill the set. He or she designs the sets, supervises the costumes, and is expected to have a good knowledge of architecture and other historical matters.

**Best boy:** assistant to the gaffer.

**Boom operator:** the person who operates the extending boom carrying the microphone to make sure it is always above the head of the actor speaking, and out of sight of the camera.

**Chief grip (key grip):** head of the team of specialised technicians who arrange the scenery on set.

**Dolly grip:** the grip who handles the camera-dolly (moving trolley) on which the camera is mounted for tracking shots.

**Gaffer:** chief electrician.

**Grip:** one of the team headed by the chief grip.

**Production manager:** the person in charge of administrating details such as salaries, transport, etc.

**Wardrobe:** the department responsible for keeping, maintaining and issuing the costumes for the production.

**Script supervisor:** the person in charge of making sure the actors know their lines, and of continuity (see page 77).

**Foley operator/editor:** someone who reproduces sound effects separately from the recording of the film.

*An 'alien mutant' in the make-up studio during the shooting of the science-fiction film,* Total Recall

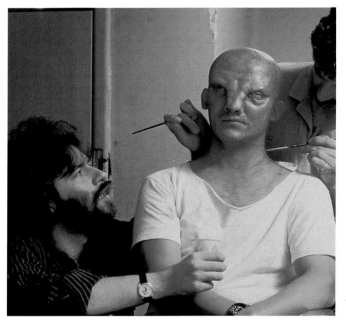

# MAKE-UP

Make-up is very important in filming. In studio sets, the presence of big lights to simulate daylight in a confined space makes the actors very hot. Any sweat or shinyness is dulled down with matt make-up and powder, and the most common call on set just before shooting is for the make-up artist to come along and apply a sponge. However, on location and outside shots, the experts say that the true art is knowing when not to use make-up. Cinema lighting strives to be as natural as possible, and there are people who need little or no make-up to look natural.

A make-up designer invents the look of the character. This may include wigs, and fake spare parts such as dental plates that are fixed to change the shape of a mouth, or facial features that are concealed or added. Make-up artists do not simply make film stars look more beautiful – they often work much harder at making them look ugly!

Particularly on period films such as *Shakespeare in Love*, make-up involves all kinds of ingredients – including dirt. Ordinary people during the reign of Elizabeth I were habitually very dirty, and even the rich and noble were not nearly as careful about bathing as most people are today. The make-up designer Lisa Westcott specialises in costume and period dramas, and was responsible for the make-up on the film. Every day of filming she mixed buckets of

## OUT TAKE

Here are a few of the make-up secrets of the big screen:

To reproduce sweat, actors are sprayed with a fine mist of glycerin and water which looks wet and does not dry out in the heat of film lights.

Rice Crispies are used, mixed with coloured gel and a skin of gelatin, to simulate the pustules of smallpox. Cornflakes pressed into a blood-coloured gelatin gel and lightly coloured with more film 'blood' make excellent scabs.

Stubble on men is produced by rubbing a layer of petroleum jelly into the actor's chin, covering it with a very fine netting known as 'hair lace', and stippling the area with finely chopped hair. The hair lace is then removed, leaving a convincing growth of 'stubble'.

A strange component of make-up is 'fish skin' – real skin from a fish – which is very strong yet easily stretched and moulded. If the make-up artist wants to disguise a healthy eye, a piece of fish skin is glued firmly above the upper lid, and then pulled down and anchored on the lower one. Fish skin glued over the lips and teased from behind with a hair clip makes wonderful 'cracked lips'.

In the film *101 Dalmatians* (1996) make-up artists were kept busy disguising each new generation of puppies (right) with fake spots so that they looked just like the puppy which started off playing the role but got too big during the period of shooting.

a grey-brown make-up called Crowe's Cremine together with grey and brown powder which settled into the cracks of people's skin and fingernails, just like real dirt. She employed a team of 40 make-up artists to get the 500 extras who played the 'groundlings' at Shakespeare's theatre bearded, dirty and sweaty and ready for filming by 8.00 each morning!

Make-up artists are often asked to reproduce the process of ageing, sometimes over a generation. A character may have to age from teens to 80s. The artists use very fine latex around the eyes and neck to simulate the wrinkled skin of older people. At other times, make-up is used to create a sex change, like Robin Williams in the film *Mrs Doubtfire* (1993). This effect was created by applying heavy make-up to the chin to cover up the stubble, and attracting attention to the eyes. Mrs Doubtfire also had a specially made set of false teeth which changed the shape of the mouth and face – and which was also used to great comic effect in one scene when they fell out.

*Robin Williams' make-up as Mrs Doubtfire included a mouthpiece to change the shape of his cheeks and body padding to change his outline.*

## CONTINUITY

Unlike plays, films are made 'out of sequence'. This means that the scenes of a film aren't necessarily shot in the order in which they finally appear on screen. Each scene is filmed by itself, and the scenes are edited together at a later date. As a result, great care must be taken to ensure that scenes filmed on different days – and sometimes in different places – match up when they are stuck together. This is the responsibility of the continuity assistant.

The continuity assistant carefully notes down details of each scene as it is made, and carries a Polaroid camera to photograph both the actor as last seen and the set as last seen to make sure they do not change. Levels of wine in a glass, for example, must be the same, or the stage reached by an on-screen meal must tie in with the last shot. An actor wearing a red dress for an outdoor shot as she walks through a hotel doorway must be wearing the same dress for the studio shot as she appears on the other side of the door – even if the two scenes were filmed several weeks apart! The result of bad continuity can be hilarious, but it can also ruin a scene. There are cinema legends about the Roman trumpeter with the wristwatch in the chariot-race scene in *Ben Hur* (1959), and the car in the background of a scene in *The Adventures of Robin Hood* (1938). Other continuity blunders include the alarm clock which goes off at 9.15 in *Four Weddings and a Funeral* (1994) when it is clearly set for 9.45, and the President's sweater in *Independence Day* (1996) which changes from dark blue to light blue in the course of one scene.

*Working in an editing suite, an editor matches the soundtrack to the lengths of film. This process is now usually done on videotape and then transferred back to film.*

# POST-PRODUCTION

Once the film has been shot, it moves into 'post-production'. At this stage, all the lengths of film that were taken during filming are spliced (joined together) and edited to make the 'final cut'. Today, this process is often done by feeding the visual information into a computer and numbering each frame so that the film can be edited on screen without having to cut and splice any actual film. This editing process is as important as shooting the film. Bad editing can turn a good performance into an embarrassingly bad film, while expert editing can sometimes rescue a poor one.

Up to this point, the only sound on the sound tape is the actors' dialogue – and some of it may not be perfect. Particularly in outside shots, there may be noises the editor does not want, or the sound quality may be poor. If this is the case, the actor re-records the affected lines, or even the whole scene, in a sound studio. The actor watches the scene and has to coincide the words exactly with the movement of his or her lips on screen.

Dubbing – adding sound after the film has been made – is also used for extra sounds, such as special effects, and music. Some sound effects come from sound libraries which contain recordings of sounds and atmospheres. But the old tried and tested sound effects are still used, such as hitting a raw cabbage with a butcher's axe to

## OUT TAKE

The film industries in Britain, America, Germany and Japan all run self-regulatory organisations to control the issue of films. Most Western censorship concerns sex and nudity, violence and extreme bad language. Censorship reflects the moral code of a particular time, for example a fashion film in 1913 was banned in the USA because it showed the models' ankles, and the 1945 historical romp, *The Wicked Lady* had to be almost entirely re-shot because star Margaret Lockwood's dresses were cut too low for American taste. Films that challenge political regimes or accepted ways of life have always been subject to censorship. Many Soviet films were banned by the Communist government, and were seen for the first time only after Mikhail Gorbachev's more relaxed 'glasnost' ('openness') policies of the 1980s. The Italian Fascist dictator, Mussolini, even banned an early (1924) version of *Ben Hur* because the Roman lost the chariot race! These days, film censors are also in charge of the release of film on videotape, and have to decide a separate video certificate rating.

produce the sound of an arrow striking home, snapping celery to simulate broken bones, or crackling cellophane to imitate the sound of fire.

The music is the last sound to be added. Some directors decide to use existing music, but many have music specially written for their film. The choice of music can make a huge difference to the effectiveness of a scene – and it need not necessarily be the music you would expect. In *2001: A Space Odyssey* (1968) Stanley Kubrick used classical music such as Johann Strauss's 'Blue Danube' to accompany the weird ballet-like motions of the docking space ship. In *Trainspotting*, Lou Reid's 'Perfect Day' accompanies a scene in which Renton (Ewan McGregor) takes an overdose. *Casablanca* (1942) uses music in a different way. The tune 'As Time Goes By' acts a kind of password for the relationship between cynical, soft-centred Rick (Humphrey Bogart) and his hopeless love, Ilse (Ingrid Bergman).

The dialogue, sound effects and music are mixed together to produce the soundtrack for the movie. The soundtrack is then laid on to the film itself in a narrow band on the left-hand side. It is read by a light-sensitive photoelectric cell which converts it into electric impulses that are fed through a decoder and broadcast through speakers.

Once this stage is completed, the film is said to be 'in the can' and it is ready for the distributor. The distributor is the middleman between studio and cinema who rents the film out to exhibitors for screening to the general public. The distributor holds 'press previews', when the film is shown to film critics and other media correspondents.

There is also the matter of film licences. Different countries have different ways of controlling the issue of films. In Britain and the USA, there are industry-backed boards of film classifiers who view each film and issue a certificate. This certificate acts as a warning to the public of the kind of sexual or violent content of the film. For example, the British Board of Film Classification has five certificates: U – suitable for children; PG – Parental Guidance advised; 12, 15 and 18 each indicating the minimum age for which the film is thought suitable. Producers and directors know the guidelines – and how to tailor their product to the rules.

*In the UK this film has been given a '15' certificate.*

## OUT TAKE

Exploitation means making the most of the public's interest in a film by selling manufactured goods connected with it. These can be as simple as baseball caps and T-shirts with slogans, or as complicated as the 'Star Wars' series of toys including light-sabres, and Darth Vader masks. Exploitation often helps keep the film in the mind of the public even after it has been out for a very long time.

# PUBLICITY

Publicity sells movies. The next most important thing after making a film is to tell the public about it. The 'pre-publicity' process starts even while the film is being made. Stories about the casting of a star appear first in the trade press – the magazines and newspapers read by people in the movie industry. But details about the film are also leaked out carefully to general newspapers and magazines. This not only prepares the audience for the forthcoming release of the film, it also helps the film-makers gauge the kind of reception the film is likely to get.

The build-up of a film, or 'hype', has been made into a fine art. One man who was an early master at hype was Alfred Hitchcock. He started to appear at least once in every film he made, usually as a passer-by or minor non-speaking part. Hitchcock was said to have made 38 appearances in his films, including appearing twice in *The Lodger* (1926). There were people who went to see each Hitchcock film as it came out, simply to be the first to spot him.

The hype for *Titanic* (1998) leaked out stories of the legendary toughness of James Cameron, the director, and the suffering of the film's stars as they were immersed in icy water for hours on end. The model of the famous liner was said to be almost as long as the real ship, and the film to take longer than the actual sinking. Once again, it worked. The film became the greatest financial success of all time, grossing more than a billion dollars, and even the musical theme was a best-seller. The trailer of *The Phantom Menace*, the 'Star Wars' prequel which picks up the story of the Jedi Knights before the story started in the 'Star Wars' trilogy, almost made the Internet melt down when 3.5 million fans all tried to view it at the same time.

## OUT TAKE

One of the best ways of attracting the public's attention to a film, once it comes out, is by pasting posters up in public places. Posters contain slogans which attempt to fix the film in the minds of the public. The poster for *The Outlaw* (1943), which introduced Jane Russell, read: 'Tall... terrific... and trouble' (left). For *Superman* (1978), the poster read: 'You will really believe you see a man fly'. The poster for *Jurassic Park* (1993) read: 'An adventure 65 million years in the making!' However, one of the best poster lines was the simple slogan for *Jaws 2* (1978): 'Just when you thought it was safe to go back in the water...'.

# THE OSCARS

The final step for a would-be movie legend is to be nominated by the Academy of Motion Picture Arts and Sciences for an Award of Merit. This Award is commonly known as an Oscar because, in 1931, a secretary at the Academy called Margaret Herrick said of the statuette: "Oh, he reminds me of my uncle Oscar!" Members of the Academy represent the various branches of film-making – for example, actors, cinematographers and film editors – and Awards are presented in more than 20 different categories. Nominations for the different categories are made by the relevant branch of the Academy, but the final winners are selected by the vote of all members of the Academy. Huge publicity campaigns accompany the whole process. In 1999, *Shakespeare in Love* and *Saving Private Ryan* were running neck-and-neck for the Best Picture Award. One of the rewards for the winner – which was *Shakespeare in Love* – is that it is said to add £40 million to the film's profits.

*Sharon Stone and companion at the glittering Academy Awards presentation ceremony in Los Angeles*

## OUT TAKE

Oscar was first awarded in 1929. Designed by art director Cedric Gibbons, and made by a sculptor called George Stanley, it is a 34-centimetre statuette of a naked man holding a sword and standing on a reel of film. Oscar is made from metal and is plated with gold.

©AMPAS®

# CINEMAS

The first cinema in the world was the Lumière brothers' converted billiard hall in the Boulevard des Capucines in Paris. It opened in 1895 (see page 17). The following year, inventor and pioneer film-maker Birt Acres opened the Kineopticon in Piccadilly, London. As the industry grew up, so did the cinema. The 1930s saw the era of the picture palace, when elaborate auditoriums were built, modelled on Egyptian temples and Spanish villages, and equipped with lounges and restaurants (see page 30).

In parts of the world where the weather is reliable, exhibitors put up screens out of doors. In India, which still has the world's largest cinema-going audience, people pay to sit on the ground in a field to see films. The first drive-in cinema was opened in Camden, New Jersey, USA, in 1933. It was a car park with a screen 12 metres by nine metres and giant sound speakers. The audience stayed in their cars. Later, RCA-Victor developed an even more sophisticated system, with speakers which could be put inside the car.

The increasing popularity of television in the 1950s was a challenge to cinema. The producers reacted with something television could not provide – size and colour – producing epic films such as *Ben Hur* (1959) and showing them on vast screens. There were also experiments with three-dimensional films, which were projected with two slightly staggered colours. The ticket price included a pair of cardboard spectacles with different coloured filters with which to view the film.

*A drive-in cinema in Beaumont, Texas, USA*

*Long queues outside the Odeon, Leicester Square in London in the 1950s*

*Wearing 3-D glasses at an Imax cinema in New York, USA*

*The film* Into the Deep *was specially made for the huge Imax screen*

The 1970s saw dwindling audiences once again. Film exhibitors started to split up their cinemas into multiples, with two, three and four screens, all working at the same time and showing different films. The idea was piloted in Britain at The Point multiplex in Milton Keynes. Within ten years the cinema-going audience in the UK doubled and the modern multiplex was born.

Imax was first launched in 1970 at the Japanese Expo 70 festival. It uses a vast, slightly concave screen to show pin-sharp pictures thrown by a 70-mm projector through which the film passes horizontally rather than vertically. In the UK, there is an IMAX cinema at the National Museum of Photography, Film & Television in Bradford as well as one just outside Waterloo Station in London, opened in 1999.

In July 1999, over 14 million people attended the cinema in the UK alone – a record attendance. But the future of cinema could be threatened by a very powerful competitor – the Internet. Already, films are being made which are released only over the Internet. As computer technology improves, and film quality and download speeds increase, this could be the next major step in the story of movie-making.

# GLOSSARY OF TECHNICAL TERMS

*Action!* The word used by the director to tell the actors, the sound recordist, and the camera operator to start a scene. Also means the contents of a filmed scene.

*Animation* The method of making inanimate objects such as puppets or cartoons, move on screen.

*Animatronics* A method of filming puppets and man-made monsters for special effects.

*Cameraman* The operative who actually takes the film.

*Cel* A sheet of clear cellulose on which the moving elements of a cartoon picture are drawn, so that the background can be seen through them.

*Censor* The person who cuts or modifies a film to prevent the showing of material thought to be too offensive.

*Choreography* The art of composing and arranging dances or fights.

*Cinematography* The art of recording a movie on film.

*Clapper board* The square, marked board with a hinged flap which is filmed at the beginning of every take to mark synchronisation of action and sound.

*Close-up* A camera shot taken from a very short distance.

*Credits* The list of cast and technicians usually shown at the end of the film.

*Cross-cut* The craft of cutting together shots of two or more different subjects filmed at different times to make them look as though they were taking place simultaneously.

*Cut!* The command given by the director to cease action and filming.

*Cutting* The craft of assembling the separate takes of a movie into a single, unified whole.

*Director* The creative person who controls the actual making of the film on the studio floor.

*Distributor* The person who takes the film from the producing company and persuades the exhibitors to show it in their cinemas.

*Dubbing* The process of adding dialogue, sound effects and music to the soundtrack of a film after the film has been shot.

*Editing* The process of choosing shots from the hundreds of 'takes' made during the filming, and sticking them together in the correct order.

*Exhibitor* The company or individual who shows the completed movie in their cinema or chain of cinemas.

*Feature* A full-length movie.

*Focus* The correct way for a camera to record a sharp, clear image on film. Sometimes deliberately blurred to give a softer image.

*Frame* A single shot from a take.

*Freeze frame* A method of stopping the action on film so that the picture is apparently 'frozen' into stillness.

*Genre* The category into which a film falls, for example, Western, comedy, horror, etc.

*Location* Real scenery, usually out of doors, which is used for filming outside the studio set.

*Long shot* The opposite of a close-up.

*Matte* Scenery painted on to glass.

*Morphing* Blending real images and special effects into one picture by the use of computer imaging.

*Newsreel* Film showing real life news, usually shown as an addition to a feature film, but also seen in special programmes in News Theatres.

*Off screen* Something that is not seen on film but which affects the story.

*Optical toys* Devices for viewing or showing moving pictures, popular before the invention of true movies.

*Panning* A shot in which a fixed camera follows the action without itself moving.

*Persistence of vision* The way in which the eye retains an image for 0.25 seconds, without which movies would be impossible.

*Prequel* A film set earlier in time than an already existing version.

*Prop* An object used to construct a scene. Small props such as handbags, guns, swords, etc. are 'hand props'. Larger, more permanent objects are 'set props'.

*Propaganda* Information, including fictional information on film, that tells only one side of a story or conflict, in order to persuade the audience of a particular version of events.

*Sequel* A film that continues the same story line as an existing version.

*Set* The scenery within which the action of a scene takes place.

*Short* A film lasting less than half an hour.

*Shot* A single continuous take, filmed from one set-up.

*Sound stage* A large, soundproof building in which sets are erected to make a movie.

*Special effects (SFX)* Effects that make the unbelievable look real on film, such as monsters, shipwrecks, fires, explosions and other technical tricks.

*Synchronise* The art of making certain that sound and action exactly match one another.

*Take* A single continuous piece of filming, giving one version of a 'shot'. A director may order any number of 'takes' before he or she is satisfied with the 'shot'.

*Talkie* A film in which the sound of the actors speaking can be heard.

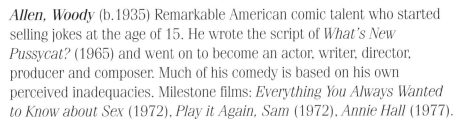

# GLOSSARY OF GREAT NAMES IN CINEMA

*Allen, Woody* (b.1935) Remarkable American comic talent who started selling jokes at the age of 15. He wrote the script of *What's New Pussycat?* (1965) and went on to become an actor, writer, director, producer and composer. Much of his comedy is based on his own perceived inadequacies. Milestone films: *Everything You Always Wanted to Know about Sex* (1972), *Play it Again, Sam* (1972), *Annie Hall* (1977).

*Balcon, Michael* (1896-1977) British producer who gave the young Alfred Hitchcock his first break. He was responsible for the Ealing comedies. Milestone films: *Kind Hearts and Coronets* (1949), *Whisky Galore!* (1949), *The Lavender Hill Mob* (1952), *The Cruel Sea* (1953), *Tom Jones* (1963).

*Bogart, Humphrey* (1899-57) American actor who after an injury in World War I was left with a scar on his face which partly paralysed his upper lip, giving him a distinctive lisp and tight-set mouth on which he quickly capitalised as a screen tough-guy. Milestone films: *High Sierra* (1941), *The Maltese Falcon* (1941), *Casablanca* (1942), *The African Queen* (1951 – Oscar).

*Broccoli, Albert 'Cubby'* (1909-96) American director who entered the movie business in 1938 as an assistant director with 20th Century Fox. Moved to England in 1950s where he produced a large number of films, he is best-known for the Bond movies. Milestone films: *Cockleshell Heroes* (1955), *The Trials of Oscar Wilde* (1960), *Dr No* (1962)

*Chaplin, Charlie* (1889-1977) see Curriculum Vitae box page 26.

*Connery, Sean* (b.1930) Scottish tough-guy who found fame with the role of James Bond and has now established himself as a leading actor. Milestone films: *Dr No* (1962 and sequels), *The Hill* (1965), *Highlander* (1985), *The Hunt for Red October* (1990), *Entrapment* (1999).

*Coppola, Francis Ford* (b.1939) American writer, director and producer who is one of the most influential movie-makers of the 20th century. Milestone films: *American Graffiti* (1973), *Apocalypse Now* (1979), *Lionheart* (1987), *The Godfather Parts II* and *III* (1974 and 1990), *The Secret Garden* (1993).

*Costner, Kevin* (b.1955) American leading actor who made a big hit with his first attempt at directing. Milestone films: *Silverado* (1985), *The Untouchables* (1987), *Dances with Wolves* (1990 also directed), *Robin Hood Prince of Thieves* (1991), *The Bodyguard* (1991), *Waterworld* (1995 – also directed).

*Crawford, Joan* (1904-77) American actress and one of Hollywood's most enduring stars and rival of Bette Davis. Milestone films: *Grand Hotel* (1932), *Mildred Pierce* (1945 – Oscar), *Whatever Happened to Baby Jane?* (1962 with Bette Davis).

*Cruise, Tom* (b.1962) American actor who studied for priesthood, but changed his mind at High School. By 1990s was the highest paid actor in the business. Milestone films: *All The Right Moves* (1983), *Top Gun* (1986), *Rain Man* (1988), *Interview with the Vampire* (1994), *Eyes Wide Shut* (1999).

*Davis, Bette* (1908-89) American actress who was a huge Hollywood star in the 1940s and 1950s. When forced to take roles she disliked, she sued Warner Bros – forcing them to take her seriously and treat her with respect. Milestone films: *Dangerous* (1935 – Oscar), *Jezebel* (1938 – Oscar), *All About Eve* (1950).

*De Mille, Cecil B.* (1881-1959) American director who was regarded as the founder of Hollywood and probably did more to make it the film capital of the English-speaking world than anyone else. Director, producer, and scriptwriter, he started his directing and producing life with *The Squaw Man* (1914). Other milestone films: *The Ten Commandments* (1956).

*De Niro, Robert* (b.1943) American actor who made a solid reputation by playing characters on both sides of the law prone to brutal violence. Owns a restaurant in Hollywood. Milestone films: *Mean Streets* (1973), *The Godfather Part II* (1974 – Oscar), *The Deer Hunter* (1978), *Raging Bull* (1980 – Oscar), *Cape Fear* (1991).

*Depardieu, Gérard* (b.1948) Youthful delinquent who turned himself into one of France's leading actors. Despite his craggy looks, he charms with ease. Milestone films: *Les Valseuses* (*The Waltzers* 1974), *Le Dernier Metro* (1980), *Jean de Florette* (1986), *Cyrano de Bergerac* (1990), *Green Card* (1990).

*Di Caprio, Leonardo* (b.1972) Baby-faced American screen star who entered films through television. Milestone films: *Critters 3* (1991), *What's Eating Gilbert Grape?* (1993), *Romeo and Juliet* (1995), *Titanic* (1997).

*Dietrich, Marlene* (1901-92) German actress who became a legend in her own lifetime, first as a sex symbol of the German cinema, and then in the USA. She was also a very successful cabaret artist. Milestone films: *The Blue Angel* (1930), *Destry Rides Again* (1939).

*Disney, Walt* (1901-66) see Curriculum Vitae box page 52.

*Eastwood, Clint* (b. 1930) American, granite-faced actor who plays action men, and also produces and directs. Made his name in TV series *Rawhide* in the 1960s, then with a series of 'spaghetti' Westerns. Milestone films: *A Fistful of Dollars* (1964 and sequels *For a Few Dollars More* 1965, *The Good, the Bad and the Ugly* 1966), *Dirty Harry* (1971 and sequels). *Firefox* (1982), *Unforgiven* (1992 – Oscar as director and producer), *The Bridges of Madison County* (1995).

*Fairbanks, Douglas Sr.* (1883-1939) see Curriculum Vitae box page 24.

*Fonda, Jane* (b.1937) American actress, daughter of actor Henry Fonda. Made several films as wide-eyed wife of Roger Vadim but her strong political views led her into more demanding roles. Milestone films: *Barefoot in the Park* (1967), *Barbarella* (1968), *Klute* (1971 – Oscar), *Coming Home* (1978 – Oscar), *The China Syndrome* (1979), *On Golden Pond* (1981 with her father).

*Ford, Harrison* (1942) American actor who once worked as a carpenter, made himself into an action man of the screen with roles like Han Solo in the 'Star Wars' films, and *Indiana Jones*. Milestone films: *Stars Wars* (1977 and sequels), *Raiders of the Lost Ark* (1981 and sequels), *Witness* (1985), *Patriot Games* (1992), *Air Force One* (1997).

*Ford, John* (1895-1973) Son of Irish immigrants to America, started work in Hollywood with his brother, Francis, appearing in *The Birth of a Nation* (1915). He formed a long working association with John Wayne. Milestone films: *The Searchers* (1956), *The Horse Soldiers* (1959).

*Foster, Jodie* (b.1962) Multi-talented American leading actress. Started acting career at age of two in commercials. First actress to win two Oscars before she was 30 (for *The Accused* 1988 and *The Silence of the Lambs* 1991). Other milestone films: *Bugsy Malone* (1976), *Taxi Driver* (1976), *Contact* (1997).

*Gable, Clark* (1901-60) American actor who starred as Rhett Butler in *Gone with the Wind* (1939) and became known as the 'King of Hollywood'. Other milestone films: *It Happened One Night* (1934), *The Misfits* (1961).

*Garbo, Greta* (1905-90) Swedish beauty who dominated Hollywood by maintaining an enigmatic silence, and taking an early retirement. Milestone films: *Anna Christie* (1930), *Romance* (1930), *Camille* (1936), *Ninotchka* (1939).

*Gibson, Mel* (b 1956) American-born actor who moved to Australia with his family, and made his name as a powerful actor in the 'Mad Max' films. Milestone films: *Mad Max* (1979 and sequels), *Lethal Weapon* (1987 and sequels), *Braveheart* (1995 – also directed).

*Goldberg, Whoopi* (b.1955) Powerful American actress who sparkles in comedy roles. First woman ever to host the Oscar ceremony (1994). Milestone films: *The Color Purple* (1985), *Ghost* (1990 – Oscar), *Sister Act* (1992 and sequel).

*Hanks, Tom* (b.1956) American actor whose one-night appearance in TV series *Happy Days* led to first casting in *Splash!* (1984) Versatile actor who has taken on a variety of dramatic roles. Milestone films: *A League of Their Own* (1992), *Sleepless in Seattle* (1993), *Forrest Gump* (1994), *Saving Private Ryan* (1998).

*Hitchcock, Alfred* (1899-1980) British director who maintained that real horror lies in not knowing when something awful is going to happen. He demonstrated this to perfection in *Psycho* (1960). Other milestone films: *Strangers on a Train* (1951), *North by Northwest* (1959).

*Hoffman, Dustin* (b.1937) American actor who first came to the attention of the film world in *The Graduate* (1967). Since then has displayed his versatility in a wide range of films. Milestone films: *Kramer vs. Kramer* (1979), *Tootsie* (1982), *Rainman* (1989).

*Hopkins, Anthony* (b.1937) Versatile and authoritative Welsh actor, inspired by late Richard Burton. Soft voice combined with raw energy make him a hypnotic screen presence. Milestone films: *The Lion In Winter* (1968), *When Eight Bells Toll* (1971), *A Bridge Too Far* (1977), *The Bounty* (1984), *The Silence of the Lambs* (1991).

*Ivory, James* (b.1928) American director who teamed up with Indian producer Ismail Merchant to produce a series of highly individual films. Milestone films: *Shakespeare Wallah* (1964), *A Room with a View* (1986), *Howard's End* (1991), *The Remains of the Day* (1993).

*Korda, Alexander* (1918-56) Born in Hungary, he started life as a journalist and soon moved into the film industry, where he made a huge impact as a director, producer and executive in Austria, Germany, the USA, France and Britain. Milestone films: *The Private Life of Henry VIII* (1933), *The Wooden Horse* (1950), *Hobson's Choice* (1953), *Richard III* (1956).

*Kurosawa, Akira* (1910-98) see Curriculum Vitae box page 48.

*Laughton, Charles* (1899-1962) See Curriculum Vitae Box page 45.

*Martin, Steve* (b.1945) American actor and former philosophy student who made the transition from stand-up comedian to light comedy to more demanding roles. Milestone films: *Three Amigos* (1986), *Roxane* (1987), *Father of the Bride* (1991).

*Méliès, Georges* (1851-1938) see Curriculum Vitae box page 18.

*Mifune, Toshiro* (1920-97) Japanese actor who combined with director Akira Kurosawa to make 16 films, including the award-winning *Rashomon* (1950). Dynamic and ferocious actor who came to be the screen face of his country. Other milestone films include: *Seven Samurai* (1954), *The Throne of Blood* (1957), *Yojimbo* (1961), *Red Sun* (1971).

*Monroe, Marilyn* (1926-62) American actress and former model who became a legend in her own lifetime Milestone films: *The Seven Year Itch* (1955), *Some Like it Hot* (1959), *The Misfits* (1961).

## WEBSITES

If you would like to find out more about the world of cinema, you could try out these website addresses:

http://uk.imdb.com/

http://www.bfi.org.uk

http://www.disney.com

http://www.wbanimation.com

*Moore, Demi* (b. 1962) American actress who made her first big break in a TV series, and went on to become one of the most glamorous stars of the 1990s. Milestone films: *Ghost* (1990), *Striptease* (1992), *Indecent Proposal* (1993), *Disclosure* (1994).

*Moreau, Jeanne* see Curriculum Vitae box page 47.

*O'Brien, Willis* (1886-1962) see Curriculum Vitae page 59.

*Paltrow, Gwyneth* (b1973) Daughter of director Bruce Paltrow and award winning actress Blythe Danner. She entered films with *Shout* (1991) and made her name as Emma Woodhouse in *Emma* (1996). Other milestone films: *Sliding Doors* (1998), *Shakespeare in Love* (1999-Oscar).

*Pfeiffer, Michelle* (b. 1957) American actress who trained as a court reporter, but won Miss Orange County beauty contest and set off for stardom. Milestone films: *Ladyhawke* (1985), *The Witches of Eastwick* (1987), *Dangerous Liaisons* (1988), *The Fabulous Baker Boys* (1989), *Batman Returns* (1992).

*Pickford, Mary* (1893-1979) see Curriculum Vitae page 24.

*Reeves, Keanu* (b.1964) American actor who was an impressive ice hockey star and devoted motor cycle rider, and became a huge success in action roles. Milestone films: *Dangerous Liaisons* (1988), *Bill and Ted's Excellent Adventure* (1989 and sequel *Bogus Journey* 1991), *Bram Stoker's Dracula* (1992), *Speed* (1994).

*Roberts, Julia* (b.1967) American actress and former model whose reputation was made by the film *Pretty Woman* (1990). Within six years was the highest paid actress in Hollywood. Other milestone films: *Flatliners* (1990), *Sleeping with the Enemy* (1991), *Mary Reilly* (1996), *Notting Hill* (1999).

*Ryder, Winona* (b.1971) Powerful and versatile American actress. Milestone films: *Beetlejuice* (1988), *Edward Scissorhands* (1990), *Bram Stoker's Dracula* (1992), *The Age of Innocence* (1993), *Little Women* (1994).

*Schwarzenegger, Arnold* (b.1947) Austrian-born, former body builder who used his magnificent physique to break into films. Milestone films: *Conan The Barbarian* (1982 and sequel), *The Running Man* (1987), *Twins* (1988), *Total Recall* (1990), *True Lies* (1994), *Batman and Robin* (1997).

*Spielberg, Steven* (b. 1947) see Curriculum Vitae box page 69.

*Stewart, James* (b. 1908-97 ) Blue-eyed American actor who specialised in honest clean-cut heroes. Remarkable performances both as a dramatic and as a comic actor. Milestone films: *Rear Window* ( 1954), *Anatomy of a Murder* (1959), *Shenandoah* (1965).

*Streep, Meryl* (b.1941) American actress who studied drama at Yale University, and went on to be a leading actress adept at everything from straight drama to black comedy. Milestone films: *The Deer Hunter* (1978), *The French Lieutenant's Woman* (1981), *Silkwood* (1983), *Bridges of Madison County* (1995).

*Taylor, Elizabeth* (b.1932) British actress who starred at the age of 10 in *There's One Born Every Minute* (1942). She won Oscars for *Butterfield 8* (1960) and *Who's Afraid of Virginia Woolf?* (1966). Other milestone films: *The Taming of the Shrew* (1967 with Richard Burton), *Cleopatra* (1968).

*Travolta, John* (b.1954) American actor who was a huge hit in *Saturday Night Fever* (1977) and then was less successful until earning an Oscar nomination for *Pulp Fiction* (1994). Other milestone films: *Look Who's Talking* (1989), *Thin Red Line* (1998).

*Valentino, Rudolph* (1895-1926) see Curriculum Vitae box page 25.

*Washington, Denzel* (b.1954) American actor who trained as a journalist but changed to stage work. By 1994 he could command more than $6 million per film. Milestone films: *Cry Freedom* (1987), *Glory* (1989 – Oscar), *Malcolm X* (1992), *The Crimson Tide* (1995), *The Siege* (1998).

*Wayne, John* (1907-79) American actor who first rose to stardom as the Ringo Kid in the Western *Stagecoach* (1939). Other milestone films: *The Searchers* (1956), *True Grit* (1969 – Oscar), *The Shootist* (1976).

*Weaver, Sigourney* (1949) American actress and producer who made her big hit as the sole survivor of a space ship harbouring an alien in *Alien* (1979). Milestone films: *Annie Hall* (1977), *Alien* (1979 and sequels), *Gorillas in the Mist* (1986).

*Williams, Robin* (b.1952) Exuberant American comedian and actor. Made his hit as fast-talking Mork in TV series *Mork and Mindy* in the late 1970s and transferred effortlessly to the big screen where he still ad-libs wildly. Milestone films: *Good Morning, Vietnam* (1987), *Dead Poets Society* (1989), *The Fisher King* (1991), *Mrs. Doubtfire* (1993), *Good Will Hunting* (1997).

*Willis, Bruce* (b.1955) American actor who made his name in the TV comedy *Moonlighting* (1985), then went on to make his mark as a tough guy. Milestone films: *Die Hard* (1988 and sequels), *The Last Boy Scout* (1991), *The Siege* (1998).

*Winslet, Kate* (b.1975) British actress, daughter of actor Roger Winslet, she was the youngest actress ever to be nominated for two Oscars (*Sense and Sensibility* 1995 and *Titanic* 1997). Other milestone films: *Jude* (1996), *Hamlet* (1996).

# INDEX